The Senses of the Text

THE SENSES OF THE TEXT

Intensional Semantics and Literary Theory

William C. Dowling

University of Nebraska Press

Lincoln & London

© 1999 by the
University of Nebraska Press
All rights reserved
Manufactured in the United States of America
⊗
Library of Congress Cataloging-
in-Publication Data

Dowling, William C.
The senses of the text: intensional semantics and literary theory
/ William C. Dowling.
p.   cm.
Includes bibliographical references (p.   ) and index.
ISBN 0-8032-1711-0 (cl.: alk. paper).—ISBN 0-8032-6617-0
(pbk.: alk. paper)
1. Semantics.   2. Semantics (Philosophy)   3. Criticism.   4. Katz,
Jerrold J.   I. Title.
P325.D68   1999
401'.43—dc21   98-36118
                                                          CIP

FOR LEO DAMROSCH

occidet Daci Cotisonis agmen,
Medus infestus sibi luctuosis
dissidet armis

Contents

Preface

This book has two aims: (1) to attempt to come at the problem of determinate meaning in literature from a new angle, and (2) to provide an introduction to the work of J. J. Katz for those in literary theory who have heard about his New Intensionalism but have also heard that it was too technical for anyone not working directly in logic or linguistics. The two aims are closely related—indeed, Katz's semantic theory *is* the new angle from which I approach determinacy of meaning—and I shall say below why this should be the case. But I want to begin by saying something about determinate meaning.

This is the notion that it is intelligible to say about a line in a poem or a sentence in a novel that it means one thing rather than another thing, X rather than Y. Forty years ago, during the period in literary studies associated with such works as Cleanth Brooks's *The Well Wrought Urn*, this was simply an axiom of literary interpretation. Today, it is customary to say, determinate meaning has been theorized away in the name of various methods or approaches that have come on the scene in the last thirty years: Derrida and *différence*, reader-response criticism, modes of "ideological" reading that take meaning to be a site of political contestation, etc.

The joker in this situation would come to light, one sees, if it turned out that determinacy of meaning were not something that could be theorized away—if, that is, like the ratio expressed by π or the primeness of prime numbers in mathematics, it existed independent of our theories and had been there all along, silently waiting for us to catch up. A growing suspicion that this may be the case has begun to make itself felt in literary studies, as when Umberto Eco, in his recent *The Limits of Interpretation*, undertakes to demonstrate that the "limit notion" of a totally mistaken or impossible interpretation derives its intelligibility from a more fundamental notion of literalness. "Within the boundaries of a given language," Eco wants now to argue, "there is a literal meaning of lexical items and that is the one listed first by dictionaries as well as the one that Everyman would first define when requested to say what a given word means" (5).

Here, already, one may glimpse the implications of Katz's intensional semantics for literary theory. For the literal meaning in search of which Eco is compelled to go to dictionaries and native speakers is, on Katz's account, something as much "inside" language as the rules of syntactic structure. As we shall see, literal meaning as Eco wants to account for it on what might be called inductive grounds is in Katz's semantics simply what occurs when type and token meaning coincide within the pragmatic or speech-act situation. Literal meaning is on this account entirely unproblematic, and as such would be a straightforward example of determinate meaning.

Yet if determinate meaning has been there all along, how did it come to be theorized away? My own sense is that this occurred because, during the period when determinate meaning functioned as an axiom in literary interpretation, it remained at the level of what Michael Polanyi called the tacit dimension of interpretive activity. Polanyi's main concern was with scientific method, but what he says transfers readily enough to other areas of inquiry, including literary interpretation. In any area of knowledge, Polanyi said—the case is made most cogently in his book *Personal Knowledge*—a great deal of the way new knowledge is acquired depends on the *observance of rules unknown as such to those following them.*

This seems on the face of it a mysterious notion. It becomes altogether less mysterious when one considers the sort of examples Polanyi offers for what he has in mind: reading the newspaper, driving a car, playing the piano. For when I am reading the evening newspaper there is an enormous complexity of rule-governed activity going on beneath the surface of my attention, even though my mind may be wholly occupied with the story I am reading. In the same way, when I am driving along the freeway I may be so absorbed in talking to you that I am scarcely aware of driving, but my driving involves a complex set of activities of which I am only partly aware. If we doubt that such operations *are* complex, all we need do, as Polanyi says, is observe the difficulties of a child just learning to read, or a student driver sitting behind the wheel for the first time.

In the period of New Criticism represented by *The Well Wrought Urn*, determinacy of meaning seems to me to have been silently assumed in just Polanyi's sense by the sort of close reading that was then assumed to be the main task of interpretation—a "rule" that guided choices between syntactic and semantic alternatives, but that was itself not felt to be subject to choice. But there is more. To go back today and follow Brooks through his reading of a Donne poem or a Wordsworth sonnet is to see that he is in each case undertaking analysis of the text as a complex speech act, a world so teeming with pragmatic implication that—for reasons I shall try to explain in chapter 5—the most sophisticated theories of pragmatic meaning developed by philosophers, by Austin or Searle or Grice or those writing under their influence, would be hopelessly inadequate to account for what is going on. This is something that the New Criticism tried to get at with its insistence on literary works as self-contained worlds with their own laws and their own logic—the "literary study of literature," as opposed to an older criticism that had viewed literary works as biographical or historical documents. Thus one was to read *Hamlet* not as evidence about the attitudes and opinions of an Elizabethan playwright named William Shakespeare, or as evidence about Renaissance beliefs—"the Elizabethan world picture," as the title of a then-popular introductory work had it—but as an imaginary world in which its protagonist is compelled by a tragic series of events to gaze into an abyss of utter meaninglessness, which is what would then explain its resemblance at a deeper level to works like Sophocles' *Oedipus Rex* in fifth-century Athens or Beckett's *Endgame* in our own time.

To look at *Hamlet* in this way is to move from the level of close reading associated with *The Well Wrought Urn* to Northrop Frye's *Anatomy of Criticism*, which, although Frye would not have thought of himself as a New Critic, may in purely theoretical terms be regarded as the summa of the formalist or New Critical program. For where critics like Brooks and theorists like W. K. Wimsatt and Monroe Beardsley had insisted on literary autonomy at the level of individual works, Frye insisted that the literary study of literature must begin in an awareness "that the existing monuments of literature form an ideal order among themselves"—he here represents himself as paraphrasing, with wholehearted approval, T. S. Eliot's *The Function of Criticism*—rather than "simply collections of the writings of individuals" (18). With the

Anatomy the theory of literary autonomy became the theory of literature as a simultaneous order of meaning. Until the arrival of Continental theory in the 1970s, Frye's notion that literary study ought to aim at "a totally intelligible structure of knowledge" about literature dominated most English departments.

Yet the *Anatomy of Criticism* seems to me also in an unexpected way to have brought about the end of New Criticism. For the sudden ascent from the Brooks level of close reading to Frye's highly abstract structural analysis—Frye's original title for the *Anatomy* was *Structural Poetics*—obscured the relation between *explication de texte* and higher-order interpretation, and in particular the way second-order interpretation derives from the analysis of primary meaning. We will discuss this matter in chapter 1. What is important here is that although Frye himself was a gifted and disciplined close reader of literary texts, as any reader of his great study of Blake's late prophecies will be aware, those whom the *Anatomy* carried suddenly up to its own stratospheric level of literary analysis were very often not.

This is the sense in which the *Anatomy of Criticism*, in dissolving the close bond between the theory of literary autonomy and a methodological emphasis on primary meaning, may be seen as having prepared the way for the current situation in English departments, which tend to be dominated by modes of "ideological" interpretation only tangentially concerned with literary study in any conventional sense. The great paradox is that Frye, in devoting his career to literature as a simultaneous order of meaning, thought of himself precisely as a defender of literary meaning against what he regarded as the reductionism of non-literary or extra-literary methods and approaches. Such approaches inevitably involve, he had said in the *Anatomy*,

> the fallacy of what in history is called determinism, where a scholar with a special interest in geography or economics expresses that interest by the rhetorical device of putting his favorite study into a causal relationship with whatever interests him less. Such a method gives one the illusion of explaining one's subject while studying it, thus wasting no time. It would be easy to compile a long list of such determinisms in criticism, all of them, whether Marxist, Thomist, liberal-humanist, neo-Classical, Freudian, Jungian, or existentialist, substituting a critical attitude for

criticism, all proposing, not to find a conceptual framework for criticism within literature, but to attach criticism to one of a miscellany of frameworks outside it. (6)

The present work does not attempt anything so grand as a theory of determinate meaning in literature. Indeed, one of its major points will be that close reading needs no theory, and even that "theory" is, when interpretation knows what it is doing, a superfluity or an encumbrance on the grounds suggested by Polanyi. My purpose, rather, is to try to show how one very powerful semantic theory permits us to see exactly what it was a gifted close reader like Brooks was doing in the days of *The Well Wrought Urn*. The notion that seems to me have gotten lost somewhere between that book and Frye's *Anatomy of Criticism* was, as I have indicated, that of literary interpretation as the analysis of a complex speech act—the lover of a Donne poem talking to his mistress, Browning's Duke talking to the emissary, Huckleberry Finn talking to an imaginary reader conjured into existence by his own discourse—such that to recover it today would be to begin moving back towards the pursuit of literary studies as a genuine discipline.

This is the project towards which Katz's New Intensionalism, especially in the period between *Language and Other Abstract Objects* and *The Metaphysics of Meaning*, seems to me to make so potentially enormous a contribution. What has kept the contribution merely potential is that Katz's theory originated in a body of technical work in Chomskyan grammar and predicate logic that is on the whole unfamiliar to literary scholars. Beyond that, the ambitiousness of his theory has compelled him over the years to engage a great deal of modern philosophy, from Frege's work in symbolic logic and the *Begriffsschrift* conception of language to Quine's arguments against the analytic-synthetic distinction to Carnap's work on meaning postulates to Lewis's possible-worlds semantics and Kripke's theory of names as rigid designators. While some people in literary theory will be acquainted with some of this work, an acquaintance with all of it cannot be expected.

In the following chapters, then, my attempt has been to present Katz's semantic theory in a way that assumes no knowledge either of Chomskyan linguistics or symbolic logic, and that fills in the philosophical background such that, for instance, the essentials of Quine's attack on analyticity or Kripke's theory of names can be followed even by those who have not read a great deal of modern philosophy. As my title indicates, this is a volume intended primarily for people in literary theory, and I have written with them in mind. Yet it perhaps goes without saying that I would pleased if some students of philosophy, at least, found the book helpful in getting a line on recent developments in Katz's New Intensionalism. Philosophical readers will find it easy to skip the portions concerned with literary interpretation or standard arguments (Frege, Quine, Kripke, Grice) in semantics and philosophy of language.

The only purely "literary" chapter is the first. For readers who have gone through their literary training in the days since *The Well Wrought Urn*, I thought it would be useful to set out one problem in "close reading" as a way of getting back in touch with a world with which they perhaps have no direct acquaintance. And then, by way of preparing for certain theoretical problems to which I return in the last chapter— primarily to show how elegantly they are solved by Katz's theory of decompositional sense structure—I thought it best to look at one or two exemplary cases in which a higher-order interpretation was shown to be untenable because it derived from misreading at the level of primary meaning. For this purpose I have taken my examples from William Kerrigan's recent discussion of several interpretations of Donne, both because Kerrigan's treatment of meaning seems to me exemplary and because his encounter with recent Renaissance criticism seems to me to be in its way a virtual parable of the state of literary studies today.

In one way or another, this book draws on conversations—one ongoing conversation, really—with friends, colleagues, and students over twenty years. I can think of no adequate way to thank those who led me to particular illuminations. I will simply list their names, and count on them to recognize their own contributions: Martin Bunzl, Linda Dowling, Frances Egan, Kit Fine, Russell Goodman, John Gordon, Richard Howard, Myra Jehlen, Peter Jones, Richard Lanham, Ruth Marcus, Robert Matthews, Alicia Ostriker, Rupert Read, Paul Ricoeur, John Searle, Fred Schueler. To discussion with a number of others, no longer alive—Morton Bloomfield, Frank Brady, Cleanth Brooks, David

Falk—I owe a great deal of my own thinking about literary theory: *advenio has miseras, magistri, ad inferias.*

Some particular debts need special mention. Over a period of years, Jerrold J. Katz has shown enormous patience with endless queries, very often obtuse, about his work. David Pitt read the manuscript with an extraordinary attention to detail, and saved me from several technical errors so major that I have subsequently repressed them. Thomas Pavel provided advice as the manuscript was going through its last revision. I am grateful to them all.

Princeton, NJ

The Senses of the Text

Over the last twenty years, perhaps no single idea in literary theory has been more under assault than the notion of determinate meaning. By this I mean simply the intelligibility of saying that a text, or a line in a poem, or sometimes a phrase or a word, means one thing and not another thing, X rather than Y. Or, to give the same idea a Popperian formulation, the idea that it is intelligible to say that a line or a word or a phrase does *not* mean X (which then may or may not count in favor of its meaning Y). In either case, the notion of determinate meaning has normally been assumed to derive from the hopelessly naive view that meaning is somehow "in" the text. This was the view in opposition to which, for instance, Stanley Fish at the beginning of his career was given to defining his posture as a reader-response critic. "The category 'in the text' is usually thought," wrote Fish at a typical moment in the late seventies, "to refer to something that is irreducibly there independently of and prior to all interpretive activities" (*TITC* 273).

Fish means this as a *reductio*: how is the concept of meaning even intelligible apart from some notion of interpretation? Yet the argument of this book, for better or worse, will be precisely that meaning exists "in the text," and that interpretation always involves reference to something that is—one could ask for no better formulation than Fish's—irreducibly there independently of and prior to interpretive activities. In particular, this will involve the claim that "meaning" as it exists for literary theory does not depend on interpretive communities, or social conventions, or language games, or ideological systems, or anything else that is, as one could say in a more innocent age, outside the text. In the last analysis, the argument would be that meanings create interpretive communities rather than the other way around.

A position so (currently) unthinkable demands a word about the terms on which it will be defended. My argument will be that the intuition that meaning is "in" the text—a powerful and persistent intuition, if one thinks about it, as witness the mighty host of modern philosophers and literary theorists who have made careers arguing against it—has been made not only intelligible but persuasive in recent years by what is now generally called the "new intensionalism" in semantic theory. Though others have made significant contributions to the project, the theorist whose work I shall take to represent the New Intensionalism is J. J. Katz, partly because his own intellectual roots go back to the Chomskyan revolution in linguistics that made the theory possible, partly because he has been taking an intensionalist line in semantics for over twenty years, and so has encountered most of the major problems and objections, and partly because *The Metaphysics of Meaning*, his most recent full-length work, gives the completest version of the theory available.

Now a caveat. In Katz's version of semantic intensionalism, meanings—"senses" is, as we shall see, the term demanded by the theory— are abstract entities. That is, they are objects existing outside the spatio-temporal-causal order in the way that many mathematicians and logicians have been led to posit the existence of things like prime numbers and sets and equilateral triangles. This position is not peculiar to Katz's theory—most people doing philosophical semantics see meanings as abstract objects—but in a post-Enlightenment world whose prime article of faith is that nothing exists or can exist outside the spatio-temporal-causal order, or that anything that might seem to is "reducible in principle" to something existing within it, this is the item that is hardest to swallow. Yet mathematical realism—roughly, the view that prime numbers are as real as tables and chairs—is a well-defended position in philosophy, and Katz's linguistic realism is, as we shall see, nothing more than an unremarkable extension of this.

I shall try to suggest in the epilogue why Katz's linguistic realism has been able to appear persuasive and even compelling to people who have seen the point of certain arguments in the philosophy of mathematics and logic. But my aim in this book will be the more modest one of adducing what I take to be the major implication of the New Intensionalism for literary theory. It is, in a word, that intensional semantics as set out in *The Metaphysics of Meaning* permits one to envision in very precise terms, and moreover to demonstrate in detail at a practical level of semantic analysis—Katz's "decompositional sense structure"—how it is possible for a linguistic system to "carry within itself" the means to say that, in a given instance of interpretation, something means X rather than Y. More, it lets one see how this might quite intelligibly occur in a way wholly independent of interpretive communities.

Since the rest of this book will be devoted to laying out the theory, I want in this chapter to say something about the stakes, as I see them, for literary interpretation. Yet here one encounters an immediate problem. So far as there has been discussion in literary theory about determinacy of meaning, it has tended to revolve around the issue of what is called the decidability of interpretation. This issue, in turn—a good example is Fish's discussion of typological readings of *Samson Agonistes* in the essay from which I quote above—has mainly been dealt with at the level of second-order interpretation. Not, in short, the level at which one talks about whether a word or a phrase means X or Y, but the level at which literary critics tend endlessly to argue, as the humorist and ex–English major Dave Barry once hilariously put it, about whether Moby Dick represents Satan or the Republic of France. For the purposes of my own discussion, the problem is that such interpretation operates at too great a remove from primary or first-order meaning— too far above the level, as one might say, where the semantic action is.

The revolution in "close reading" associated with New Criticism in the fifties, on the other hand, provided a great deal of semantic action at this level, but very little theory. (Wimsatt and Beardsley and others normally read as theorists of New Criticism are best regarded, in my view, as having written in defense of a very powerful *method*—more precisely, of the way the literary work is posited or projected as an object of inquiry by that method.) This is why, if one today goes to the library in search of books on the indeterminacy of literary meaning, one finds the shelves crowded with recent entries in the field. To go looking for a comparable body of work on determinacy of meaning, on the other hand, is to search in vain. The shelves are bare. If one discounts such specimens as Hirsch's *Validity in Interpretation*, which belong to older controversies about authorial intention, the best one can generally hope to turn up is a battered copy of Brooks and Warren's *Understanding Poetry*.

The absence of strong theoretical thinking on the side of determinacy is today felt most acutely, no doubt, by those who have for whatever reason refused to abandon the notion of determinate meaning in their teaching. For it is in the classroom that the bareness of the theory shelves translates most immediately into a sense that one is lonely and isolated in maintaining that a certain word or phrase means X rather than Y. My own solution to the problem over the years has been to compose for my students handouts that try to show, in a more systematic way than classroom discussion permits, how close reading sustains and is sustained by the principle of determinate meaning. They have been, I must ruefully admit, written partly out of self-protection. When indeterminacy is in the air, and when one's colleague teaching the literature class across the hall may very well be conducting an hour of collective free association, the notion that some readings are misreadings must expect to encounter undergraduate resistance.

That is part of the story, but not all of it. To get at the rest, I should like to look briefly at one example of these classroom handouts. Its occasion was a stanza of Donne's *Valediction: Forbidding Mourning*, or rather a misreading of the stanza by a substantial portion of the class:

> Moving of th'earth brings harms and fears,
>   Men reckon what it did and meant;
> But trepidation of the spheres,
>   Though greater far, is innocent.

The class was English 219 at Rutgers University, an introductory course in poetry required of all prospective English majors. The students were at this point developing fast as close readers—none, for instance, made the "normal" undergraduate mistake of taking *compasses* in a later stanza to refer to magnetic compasses—and all had been trained in use of the OED. The misreading, as most people who have taught the poem will have guessed, concerns *moving of th' earth*, which more than half the class had taken to refer to planetary motion (with two subgroups, one opting for the earth's motion around the sun, the other for its rotation on its own axis). This was the handout:

HOW WAS I SUPPOSED TO KNOW THAT WAS AN EARTHQUAKE?
—A PROBLEM IN CLOSE READING

Last week, we discussed Donne's *Valediction*. When we got to a certain stanza, about half of you understood our in-class analysis— you had seen on your pensum exercise that *moving of th'earth* must refer to an earthquake—and everybody else was mystified: how in the world were we supposed to know that the speaker is talking about *earthquakes* here? Since the whole stanza is obviously about planets and planetary motion, and since the earth is a planet, why couldn't an intelligent reader take *moving of th'earth* to refer, say, to the earth's motion around the sun? (There even is an OED definition that refers specifically to the motion of the planets: how were we supposed to know it didn't refer to the motion of the earth as a planet?) These are good questions. Let's look at the stanza that caused the trouble:

> Moving of th'earth brings harms and fears,
>   Men reckon what it did and meant;
> But trepidation of the spheres,
>   Though greater far, is innocent.

Now by the time we had finished discussing this stanza, we had decided that it meant something like the following: "Earthquakes, when they happen, cause physical damage or *harms* (buildings collapse, bridges come tumbling down) and *fears* (people get nervous or anxious when they feel the walls shaking). When the earthquake is past, men *reckon* or try to calculate the damage (*what it did*) and if there is any portent involved (*what it meant*: in earlier societies, an earthquake could be taken as a sign that the gods, or God, was angry about something). But irregularities in the motion of the moon and planets around the earth (*trepidation of the spheres*), though they involve the movement of huge celestial bodies, are never taken to be damaging or threatening (*innocent* here has its older meaning of "not giving harm or damage"].

My parallel for what the speaker is saying, you may remember, asked you to think for a second about our modern notion of the earth as a planet in motion around the sun. If you were in an automobile going 600 miles an hour, you would be terrified. (This is like the *moving of th'earth* in the poem: a movement that involves you locally, and therefore scares the hell out of you.) But *in fact* you are right now traveling at a much faster speed (66,587 mph)— that's the speed at which the earth is hurtling around the sun as you read this sentence—and you feel perfectly calm. The cosmic motion occurs on so vast a scale that you don't notice it. That's exactly what the speaker of Donne's *Valediction* is saying in the stanza above, except the solar system he's thinking of is the old Ptolemaic one in which the earth sits motionless at the center of the universe and everything else (sun, moon, planets, stars) moves around it.

How are you supposed to know any of that, or figure it out? Well, start with the syntax of the line—it's the *grammar* of the speaker's sentence that's going to tell you how to work through to earthquakes and planetary motion here. Suppose you've read and reread the stanza, and you don't know what it means, and you haven't even tried to look up anything in the OED yet. There is something you can figure out, though, just by looking at the syntax of the line: *one thing is being compared or contrasted to another thing.* How do you know that? Look again at the last two lines of the stanza, this time paying attention to the italicized words:

> *But* trepidation of the spheres,
> Though *greater* far, is innocent.

Now look at the use of *but* in that line, and you will realize that *but* in this situation is always used in English to imply a comparison or contrast, e.g.,

> Susan is a good student *but* Harry is better.
> I'd like to live in Florida *but* I'd rather live in Maine.
> I love Donne's poetry *but* I love Browning's more.

Now back to the original line. Even though we don't know yet what the words mean, we do know that we're entitled to look for some sort of contrast here:

> *Moving of th'earth* [is X] BUT *trepidation of the spheres* [is Y].

Now look at the word *greater. Greater* is what is called a comparative, but you don't need to know that to know (as a native speaker of English) that whenever you run across it, something is being compared to something else. Again, compare:

> George is tall, but Harry is *taller.*
> Peter is smart, but Susan is *smarter.*

Okay so far? Now notice something else: whenever you compare two things, there must be something they have in common to be subject to comparison. When you say "George is tall, but Harry is taller," for instance, you are comparing George and Harry with respect to one quality, namely, their height. Notice, by the way, that when two things *don't* have something in common, comparison between them sounds silly or absurd:

George is tall, but Sally is Catholic.

In the Donne stanza, then, what we are trying to zero in on is some common feature or shared quality of *moving of th'earth* and *trepidation of the spheres* in virtue of which they are being compared with each other. Now let's pause and use our heads for a second. Since *moving* is a word that we already know to have something to do with motion or movement—"I see something moving behind that tree over there"—the word we obviously want to pin down is *trepidation*. This too is a word with a number of modern meanings ("George felt some trepidation when he saw his boss walk into the room"), but none of them seem to have anything to do with *spheres*, which are globes or circles of some sort. So let's go to the OED and see if we can find a meaning for *spheres* that would permit them to be imagined as something subject to movement or *trepidation*. When we do this, one meaning will stand out right away:

Sphere. 2. One or other of the concentric, transparent, hollow globes imagined by the older astronomers as revolving around the earth and respectively carrying with them the several heavenly bodies (moon, sun, planets, and fixed stars).

This seems promising because, along with giving us a complete picture of the earth in relation to the planets (as understood in Renaissance astronomy), it also involves the notion of movement (*revolving, carrying with them*) needed for the comparison we've isolated.

Let's assume for a minute, then, that the *spheres* are the cosmic spheres in OED def. 2. Then what could *trepidation* be? When we look this word up in the OED, one definition leaps right off the page:

Trepidation. 3. *Astron.* [This means "used as a term in astronomy."] A libration of the eighth (or ninth) sphere, added to the system of Ptolemy by the Arab astronomer Thabet ben Korrah, c. 950, in order to account for certain phenomena.

(Here you make a discovery: one of the OED examples used to illustrate this meaning of *trepidation* is the very line from Donne that we're trying to figure out. So we must be in the immediate vicinity of the correct meaning.)

Here you are at a fork in the road. All you really need to figure out the stanza at this point is a rudimentary idea of what the Ptolemaic universe looked like—the system of a fixed earth and nine spheres that people believed in from ancient times until the sixteenth and seventeenth centuries, when Copernicus, Kepler, Galileo, and then Newton made discoveries and calculations that convinced everyone that the earth was *not* fixed or motionless, but that it was a relatively small planet moving around the sun in a relatively unimportant solar system. (The new discovery of the so-called heliocentric universe did a lot to humble human pride. Earth and humankind were no longer the center of God's creation, but just a tiny part of an immense physical universe. This is a process you can trace in intimate and dramatic detail in English literature between Chaucer and Pope.)

The obvious way to figure all this out, and the one I most highly recommend, is to take half an hour, go to the library, and read up in the *Encyclopedia Britannica* (11th edition) under "Ptolemy" or "Galileo." If you do this, you will (1) be figuring out this stanza in Donne, (2) acquiring an image of the universe indispensable to understanding ancient and modern literature through the Renaissance (the universe of this Donne poem is also the universe of Chaucer, Dante, Shakespeare, and hundreds of other major and minor writers), and (3) adding to your own knowledge as an educated woman or man. This is a pretty big payoff for 30 or 45 minutes' reading.

If you are in a hurry, though, you can simply look up *libration* in the OED definition above, to see if it refers to the kind of movement the speaker has in mind. And it does:

"**Libration**. 2. *Astron.* A real or apparent motion of an oscillating kind. *Libration of the moon*: an apparent irregularity of the moon's motion which makes it appear to oscillate."

Let's take a moment to see where we are. Since we know that *trepidation of the spheres* refers to the motion of the planets around the earth in the Ptolemaic system, we know that we've arrived at something like the following: "The movement of the planets around the earth, though greater far than *moving of th'earth* [whatever that turns out to be] does not make people anxious or afraid."

So in *moving of th'earth* we are looking for something that— in contrast to the silent and orderly movement of the planets— makes people anxious or afraid (*brings harms and fears*, makes *men reckon what it did and meant*, etc). So let's scan the possible OED definitions under *moving* to see if we can find one that might lead to fear or anxiety. Immediately, we will notice this one:

> *Moving.* 1. Changing of place or position; stirring, motion, movement.

What's just as interesting is that, among the OED examples given for this definition is one from a book published about the same time as Donne's poem that says that this kind of *moving* could be a tremor:

> 1620 Barrough. *Meth. Physick.* Tremor is a disease that is accompanied with two sundry movings.

Now we have seen, presumably, two things: (1) as a violent motion or *tremor*, this kind of *moving of th'earth* stands in clear contrast to *trepidation of the spheres* as a silent, orderly planetary motion, and (2) we already have an ordinary or everyday word for just this sort of tremor—*earthquake.* So we try paraphrasing the original stanza as indicated at the beginning: "Earthquakes cause fear or dismay, but planetary motion, though occurring on a far vaster scale, goes wholly unnoticed." *Now* we are (at last!) in a position to discuss the more important meaning of this stanza, which is what it implies about the relationship between the speaker and the woman he is addressing. (He is, you will recall, going on a journey, and she is unhappy about their being apart for weeks or months. He is trying to get her to see that the parting of "dull sublunary lovers" is accompanied by a lot of violent upheaval, just like earthquakes, while *their* love, being higher and more spiritual and perfect, allows them to part silently and peacefully, like the planets in their cosmic motion.)

But suppose you had a reader who didn't see any of this, even after you had pointed out the relevant facts about the Ptolemaic theory of the universe and the relevant *OED* definitions? Suppose such a reader were to say, for instance, "I still don't get it. Since the whole thing is about planetary motion, and since the earth is a planet in motion around the sun, I think *my* reading, which is that *moving of th'earth* refers to the motion of the earth as a planet, is just as good as your reading, which is that *moving of th'earth* means 'earthquake'."

This is the kind of disagreement that can come up even with very bright students, and it is the kind of thing a class like 219 has to be convincing about if "close reading" is to be taught as the basis of literary interpretation. In this case, how exactly would you go about convincing such a reader that *moving of th'earth* means "earthquake" and not "movement of the earth as a planet"?

The answer, as you probably have figured out, lies in directing the other student's attention to *trepidation of the spheres* and pointing out that the only possible meaning for *spheres* here is the heavenly spheres that contain the sun, moon, and planets in the Ptolemaic system. (If you can't get him or her to accept this, then there really isn't any hope of agreement: all interpretation has to start from some commonly agreed upon basis of knowledge. But most students who have been taught how to use the *OED* and an encyclopedia will readily see that *spheres* here must be Ptolemaic spheres.) Now you have a knockdown argument in your favor: (1) "earthquake" makes perfect sense in this context because it fits the controlling contrast or comparison implied by *but* and *greater* while (2) "movement of the earth as a planet around the sun" doesn't make sense **because in the Ptolemaic system the earth does not move around the sun: it is the fixed or motionless center of the universe.** So the only plausible candidate for the meaning of *moving of th'earth* is the more local phenomenon of an "earthquake," and when you've seen that, everything else in the stanza fits.

The part of the story that remains to be told concerns student response to such handouts. For the curious and important fact is that, as students get more expert at syntactic analysis and using the *OED*, resistance to the idea of determinate meaning fades totally away. The colleague across the hall might, I grant, enter objections at this point—that this is simply a form of collective free association regimented by the OED, or that a class in how to make astrological prognostications might report similar "progress"—but I do not want to pause over them. The rest of this book is meant as an answer to that sort of objection. I do want to consider, however, what seems to me overwhelmingly likely to be the real explanation of the phenomenon, which is that it is the *method*—a certain way of reasoning from a tacit knowledge of syntactic and semantic rules to hypotheses about meaning—that is doing the convincing.

The reason that first-order meaning as discussed in the *Valediction* handout assumes major importance in the current theoretical climate, it seems to me, is that it suggests a solution to the otherwise intractable problem of opposing or conflicting second-order interpretations. For, as Stanley Fish shrewdly saw in using such conflicts as evidence for his own position on interpretive communities, there simply is no obvious way of arbitrating disagreement at the higher level. Given opposing second-order interpretations of Blake's *The Tyger* or Milton's *Samson Agonistes*, one's best bets seem to be either to declare for a somewhat lax critical pluralism—Moby Dick as both Satan *and* the Republic of France, as it were—or (Fish's line in *Is There a Text in This Class?*) to declare meaning determinate in relation only to some interpretive community that shares certain deep-level assumptions.

This is a situation that alters radically when first-order meaning enters the picture. For now the crucial consideration is that, in any case of opposing second-order interpretations, the critic who can show that his or her opponent has misread the words on the page holds a trump. I want to look in some detail at one example of this principle in operation, taken from an essay in which William Kerrigan is discussing recent work in seventeenth-century literature. The venue is the MLA volume *Redrawing the Boundaries*, in which contributors had been asked to summarize recent developments in their fields. In the background of Kerrigan's discussion, no doubt, lies a general intuition that second-order interpretation derives in a rule-governed way from hypotheses about first-order meaning, and accordingly stands or falls with them. But my point will be that one does not need the story to know when the trump has been played.

Kerrigan's essay discusses, as does my student handout, a poem by

Donne. The example this time is *Elegy XIX* ("To His Mistress Going to Bed"), which used to be read as one of Donne's religion-of-love poems, a celebration of sexual consummation—here, the prospect of it—in terms normally reserved for religious transcendence. Thus the speaker of the poem, whose lady has been slower in unclothing herself than he, urges her in playfully extravagant terms to expedite matters: *Now off with those shoes, and then safely tread / In this, love's hallowed temple, this soft bed. / In such white robes heaven's angels used to be / Received by men.* The opening lines of the poem have been the occasion of much recent discussion, mainly, one surmises, because matters of sexuality have a special fascination for gender criticism, and the simile of a soldier tired with standing on alert while awaiting engagement with the enemy contains a punning joke about the speaker's erection:

> *Come, Madam, come! All rest my powers defy;*
> *Until I labor, I in labor lie.*
> *The foe oftimes, having the foe in sight,*
> *Is tired with standing, though he never fight.*

The source of Kerrigan's annoyance is, as we shall shortly see, a kind of interpretive free association authorized by certain recent approaches, specifically (in this case) gender studies. But his deeper point will be that such interpretation, usually assumed by its enemies to testify to the baleful influence of Derrida or Lacan, begins from something much humbler and closer to home, what in the days of Brooks and Warren would have been called misreading pure and simple. This is why, one suspects, Kerrigan elects to begin his discussion with John Carey's *John Donne: His Life and Art.* For Carey, though no doubt greatly influenced by recent work in gender studies and feminist criticism, is without theoretical pretensions. Here is his account of *Elegy XIX*: "The despotic lover here, ordering his submissive girl-victim to strip, and drawing attention to his massive erection (the point of Donne's jokes about 'standing'), is of course a perennial dweller in the shadow-land of pornography, particularly attractive as a fantasy role to males who, through shyness or social circumstance, find relations with women difficult" (qtd. in Kerrigan 69).

Kerrigan's response to this is peremptory, appealing to syntax and semantics and literary history all at once, but what carries the day is his relentless emphasis on primary meaning. So, for instance, Kerrigan duly notes the agreement of all commentary on the poem that *standing* in line 4 involves a joke about an erection. "But whence 'massive'? . . . No size is stipulated, and 'tired with standing' seems to convey, if anything, a fear that the erection, whatever its current size, will lapse if they do not proceed." (The ellipsis is Kerrigan's somewhat plaintive appeal to literary history: "I cannot think of an English poet of the period who *does* mention the size of his penis except Campion, and the point of his epigram is that he would have been more successful with a smaller one.") In the same way, Kerrigan plays the trump of primary meaning against what he calls Carey's silly generalizations about pornography. Isn't the poem, he asks, in part about "the frustration of seeing as opposed to the joys of touching and doing?" Then (trump): "Does one address a 'girl-victim' as 'Madame'?" (69).

I will say in a moment why I think the emphasis on primary meaning works so powerfully here, but let us first look briefly at another interpretation of *Elegy XIX* discussed by Kerrigan, this one a more self-consciously "theoretical" exercise in poststructuralist reading. Kerrigan's point is going to be that something quite extraordinary is occurring here, namely, that this second critic (Thomas Docherty) is taking as his point of departure not Donne's text but Carey's earlier musings about the speaker's "massive erection" and the strip tease of his "girl-victim." The ingredients of Docherty's interpretation will be, therefore—it is an exemplary moment for anyone who wants to understand literary studies as they have developed over the last twenty years— (1) Carey's rescripting of the poem as a pornographic fantasy, followed by (2) a bit of free-form fantasizing about the lines in which the speaker is telling his lady (*Off with that girdle, like heaven's zone glittering / But a far fairer world encompassing*) to hurry with taking off her girdle. Here is Docherty:

> The *girdle* "contains" the *girl,* and the breach made in this girdle to "produce" the girl becomes tantamount to a breach in the body of the girl herself, tantamount to the opening of the girl's legs, her "compass." . . . The opening of this "compass" or world, and the subsequent re-encompassing not of the girl herself but of the male in the circle described by the embrace of the girl's legs, constitutes the enactment of the rupture of the "girl" [both word and person] in the breaking of her hymeneal boundary. (qtd. in Kerrigan 70)

Kerrigan's response is once again peremptory: "'Madame' is not a virgin, and Donne nowhere addresses a 'girl'." Not that he fails to register a more generalized annoyance—"What we have here is a critic fantasizing about Carey's fantasies about the poem" (70)—but this, I want to suggest, would count for nothing if he had not been able to demonstrate, at once economically and conclusively, that both interpretations rest on simple misreadings. This is what brings the entire dispute down to a matter of meaning as governed by syntactic and semantic rules. Thus, for instance, *tired of standing*. May *stand* mean "erect" in the sexual sense? (Yes: "applied to *penis erectus*," Partridge, *Shakespeare's Bawdy*). Is there any textual evidence that the speaker's erection is, or that he sees it as being, "massive"? (No.) Where does the suggestion that it is "massive" come from? (See "Carey's fantasies" just above.) Similarly, "girl-victim," "strip," "embrace of the girl's legs," "hymeneal boundary," etc.

The moral of the tale lies in the glimpse it permits of language as an abstract system of rules—L, as it is sometimes symbolized by linguists—and, beyond that, as a system existing separate from speakers and readers. For Carey and Docherty represent contemporary interpretation in a familiar aspect, as a burgeoning structure of second-order inference that has come unmoored from "meaning" as determined by syntactic and semantic rules. The reason that any emphasis on primary meaning works as a trump in this situation is that it insists, beyond the local dispute about a word or a phrase, on the independent validity of such rules. Kerrigan trumps his opponents, in short, not by out-arguing them but by conducting his own argument in a way that simply permits him to step aside, leaving the misreadings of Carey and Docherty in a direct confrontation with language-as-L.

To look at the same episode from the viewpoint of Carey or Docherty, on the other hand, is to see why the notion of meaning as inseparable from interpretive community is so essential to the way they are attempting to read Donne. For if readers who reason from syntactic rules and lexical meaning simply represent one interpretive community among others, Kerrigan has no trumps to play. This gives us the sense in which Kerrigan's argument must, quite apart from his own views or intentions—I have no idea, I should say, of Kerrigan's views on determinacy or indeterminacy of meaning—assume the existence of language as a system wholly independent of those who use it. (As we

shall see, Katz makes a similar argument about Chomsky's competencism—i.e., that formal theories of language in the Chomskyan tradition must be understood as positing language as existing separate from
its speakers, though Chomsky himself has had great difficulty accept-
ing this.)

I will end by saying a word about the idea of language with which
this leaves us—the vision of what Katz at an earlier point in his career
liked to call "language as an abstract object"—but I want to note in
passing an issue concerning interpretive community that I shall post-
pone discussing until some theoretical groundwork has been laid. It
concerns Fish's usual mode of arguing, some years ago, for the primacy
of interpretive community. The essential move was, as we shall see in
detail later, to shift questions into a pragmatic or speech-act context
where extra-linguistic considerations silently take over from language-
as-such the role of determining "meaning." One version of this move
was to concentrate on short utterances—"The suit is too light to wear"
is a canonical example—for which a variety of speech-act contexts can
be imagined. Another was to equate language purely and simply with
social convention. (Fish's best-known example: a student in a seminar
raises his hand. Within the "interpretive community" of the seminar,
this signifies a desire to speak. But a visitor from another culture might
think the student was warning the class that the ceiling is about to
fall in.)

My main reason for postponing consideration of this issue is that
Katz's system is, so to speak, more than ready to take on this kind of
argument. As we shall see, the New Intensionalism is particularly ele-
gant in the way it handles speech pragmatics, from standard Austin-
Searle speech-act theory to Gricean conversational implicature to (perhaps) the Wittgensteinian doctrine of meaning as use. But a subordinate reason is to register my sense that, in leaving Fish's arguments
until later (chapter 5), one is not ducking any really crucial issues.
From the perspective of intensional semantics, the whole problem
with arguments that begin by equating language with social conventions—raising one's hand in a class, driving on the right rather than
the left—is that they beg the question of meaning in an essential way.
For such examples *are* examples of non-linguistic social convention,
and the whole question is precisely whether language is something
over and above a system of such conventions.

As will be evident by now, my own views on language and meaning are wholly opposed to the notion that interpretive community plays any essential role in the matter. Indeed, I want quite seriously to defend the position that the words and sentences and syntactic rules of a language—and therefore every potentially meaningful utterance in that language, and therefore the meaning of those utterances—could in an intelligible sense be said to exist even if there existed not a single human being who spoke or understood it. For Katz, whose unabashed linguistic Platonism has room even for languages that no one on earth will ever speak and no earthling will ever imagine—those languages, as he might say, exist in the same "place" that, for instance, French existed in 2000 B.C.—this presents no particular problem. For me, given the more limited aims of this book, the problem lies in getting across the intuition that permits one to "see" how language could exist independent of interpretive community.

It is not an easy intuition to get across. Over the years, the example that has come to seem to me most illuminating is the Rosetta Stone, or rather the ancient language encoded in the Egyptian hieroglyphic writing that the Rosetta Stone restored to a sudden miraculous legibility at the beginning of the nineteenth century. To take seriously the notion that meaning depends on interpretive community—or social conventions, or language games, or whatever—would be, at an extreme, to take seriously the notion that during the long centuries that the hieroglyphs had gone silent the ancient language encoded in them had quite literally ceased to exist as a language, that the hieroglyphs themselves had been reduced to nothing more than arbitrary scratchings. This is not an absurd view. To the contrary, there is a tree-falls-in-the-forest quality to the problem of the silent hieroglyphs that can, if one is in the right frame of mind, make any other view appear absurd.

My contention in the following pages, however, will be that the view wholly opposed to this has a great deal to recommend it—that, when we have understood its relation to the entire structure of our knowledge and our own existence as conscious or rational beings, the opposing view is in fact the truer one. This is the view that, during the long centuries when the hieroglyphs had gone silent, the ancient language encoded in them may in a wholly intelligible sense be said to have existed as a language, with its morphemes and words and sentences and syntactic and semantic rules and all the meanings—"senses," to hold to Katz's intensionalist terminology—made possible by these in their totality. The ancient language would on this view simply and contingently have been one originating among a community of speakers who subsequently vanished from the earth.

From the viewpoint of intensional semantics, the Rosetta Stone example has the great virtue of permitting us to keep in view the vision of language—and, in the ontological distance behind it, the abstract entities known as senses—that Katz projects as the necessary consequence of an adequate semantic theory. It is also, as I shall subsequently argue, a vision made wholly persuasive by Katz's interpretation of the type-token relation, whether or not one accepts his linguistic Platonism. For one may easily enough imagine oneself, no matter what one's theory of meaning, standing before the hieroglyphs during the long stretch of time when they had gone silent, knowing full well that a language was there if one could see through to it. The lesson for literary theory is obvious. It will be that when we are reading Donne's *Valediction: Forbidding Mourning* or *Elegy XIX* we have encountered a domain of meanings or senses wholly independent of our interpretation—they would be there even if we and every other speaker of English were to vanish tonight—and that it is this domain to which reading and interpretation is ultimately responsible.

The example of Donne's *Valediction* in the last chapter calls into play, I take it, certain persistent intuitions about language and meaning—e.g., that the students who went to the OED to look up *trepidation* and *spheres* weren't involved in some random activity like casting the *I Ching*, or that there were rules of relevance to guide their selection of some definitions over others. And behind these intuitions lie deeper ones: that the OED can intelligibly be viewed, for instance, as a repository of actual English meanings or senses, or that syntactic function may assign quite different meanings to words—*home*, say, as a verb rather than a noun—otherwise identical in form. One major significance of intensional semantics for literary theory lies in the way it backs up such intuitions.

Even when they have been backed up, as we shall see, a number of logical and philosophical problems remain. We will look at these in later chapters. But I want to begin by trying to give a sense of the way in which Katz's New Intensionalism comes at the problem of meaning—this is intensionalism, once again, as the theory that meanings are actually "in" language, and more particularly that words may contain multiple senses as part of their semantic structure—as well as some preliminary intimation of how he will counter the powerful movement in modern philosophy (Quine, Goodman, Davidson) that says that the very concept of "meaning" is the ghostly residue of an exploded metaphysics. (The equivalent in the modern age, as Quine famously said, of Homer's gods.)

The great modern exponent of this view is Wittgenstein, to whose *Philosophical Investigations* Katz devotes the longest chapter of *The Metaphysics of Meaning*, concentrating especially on Wittgenstein's analysis of an utterance—"Slab!"—used to illustrate the idea that meaning derives from use. Katz's discussion of this example has already begun to draw philosophical attention (see Levvis), and it is easy to see why. Wittgenstein's "deflationary" account of meaning-as-use is the single most influential attempt so far to dispel the notion of linguistic meanings as autonomous entities, and Katz is the best-known modern exponent of a linguistic realism—"semantic Platonism," as Levvis calls it—that insists on their real existence. (I shall use *linguistic realism* to refer to the doctrine that linguistic entities have a real existence independent of language users, in the way mathematical realism understands prime numbers or equilateral triangles to have a real existence separate from mathematicians. Katz quotes, in this connection, the great Cambridge mathematician G. H. Hardy: "I believe that mathematical reality lies outside us, that our function is to discover or *observe* it, and that the theorems which we prove . . . are simply our notes of our observations" [*LOAO* 22–23]).

Since Katz emphasizes the resemblance between his own linguistic realism and Hardy's mathematical Platonism, it can be tempting to see him as a Platonist tout court—that is, as someone who has begun by assuming that certain linguistic entities exist outside the spatiotemporal realm, and who then wants to try to solve certain problems (analyticity, entailment, etc) on this basis. There are further reasons for looking at Katz this way. For instance, he will always point out that his own semantic theory, like that of Chomsky at the syntactic level, involves a "top-down" model of meaning: constraints are seen as being imposed on actual utterance by linguistic rules existing outside the speech-act situation. Then, related to the "top down" model, is an interpretation of the type/token relation central to Katz's entire theory. He standardly introduces this by citing a passage from C. S. Peirce:

> There will ordinarily be about twenty "the"s on a page, and of course they count as twenty words. In another sense of the word "word," however, there is but one "the" in the English language; . . . it is impossible that this word should lie visibly on a page or be heard in any voice. (qtd. in *MM* 39)

Against this background, it is essential to see that Katz's New Intensionalism, though it will indeed end as a fully developed linguistic realism, does not begin in some timeless world of Platonic archetypes. It begins at the level of actual speech or utterance. Consider, for instance, the idea of speech implied by Peirce's account. If we concentrate on type-meaning—the *the* that cannot be heard in any voice or seen on any page—the Platonic overtones are obvious. But if we think for a moment about the token or utterance level—the level at which I actually make bursts of noise in the air or marks on paper to communicate with you—it is clear enough that something like a type/token distinction is needed simply to account for what most of us do most of the time.

By talking about any given occurrence of "the" in my speech or writing as a *token* of an ideal *type*, Peirce simply wants to insist on its contingency. I may use "the" twenty times, or forty, in talking to you on the telephone or writing you a letter, but no great leap is involved in imagining a world in which I did not exist—as would have happened had I been run down by a truck last Tuesday, say—or you did not exist, or this particular conversation had never taken place. The same is true of every conversation: it occurs within a given spatio-temporal context (Princeton, early morning, July 17), and the world might have been so arranged that it never happened at all. Yet the *the* that existed as an abstract possibility of English meaning before you and I were born, and will exist after we are gone, is unaffected by any of this. It is a permanent type of which any actual utterance of ours must be simply and contingently a token produced on some particular occasion.

So far, however, it is not clear that we need to leap to Peirce's realm of ideal types to explain what is going on. The meaning of "the" might, as on Wittgenstein's account, simply arise from its use in a language game, which would then make Peirce's account a perfect example of metaphysics in the "bad" sense: what happens when, as often occurs, we start conjuring up invisible entities to explain what is going on right before our eyes. This is why Katz, in a way that is much closer to an unmixed empiricism than any full-blown Platonism, will always go to such lengths to insist that his linguistic realism does not begin from some underlying system of Platonic assumptions about language and reality. It begins, rather, from just watching what happens when we speak.

Consider an ordinary but for-that-very-reason-usually-unremarked aspect of normal speech or utterance: few of us are so articulate that we just come right out and speak in perfectly formed English sentences. What more normally happens is that our linguistic utterance occurs amidst a welter of non-linguistic elements. The speaker may be, for instance, shy or hesitant:

I was, um, on my way to, er, the store when, um . . .

Or the articulatory mechanism may have been so constructed as to produce a stutter:

I w-w-w-w-was on m-m-m-my way to the s-s-s-s-store when . . .

Or the speaker may be an American teenager talking to a friend:

I was, like, on my, like, way to the, like, store when, like . . .

Or, as Katz says, the speaker may be drunk (much slurring of syllables), or unpardonably rude (belches, burps), or so agitated or excited that words get needlessly repeated, and so on.

This is the situation in which Peirce's account stops looking like Platonic speculation and begins to look more like a model for understanding what actually goes on in human utterance. For it is a fact that in any of the situations above we will normally pick out certain elements—the ones that compose the sentence *I was on my way to the store when I ran into Sally*—as being meaningful while ignoring others (slurrings, stutters, belches) as being irrelevant to the speaker's meaning. And it is very difficult to say that what we are *not* doing in this situation is "hearing" a top-down type-token relation between certain elements and recognizing that with others this relation is missing or absent. So it is, on an intensional account, that we hear a meaningful sentence amidst the non-linguistic clutter.

Now Wittgenstein will have none of this, of course, which is why it falls to Katz's lot to show that the various ways in which Wittgenstein counters the notion of "meaning" as an entity with an alternative notion of meaning-as-use are all in some sense deficient—and more, that they are deficient in ways for which only an intensional theory of meaning can fully account. The long (112-page) chapter in *The Metaphysics of Meaning* where Katz discusses the *Philosophical Investigations* is a single extended episode in which the two systems are intentionally brought into collision. It is the way Katz then picks up the pieces—what is left, so to speak, when Wittgenstein's notion of meaning-as-use has been given its full due and one sees that there remains a great deal to be explained—that constitutes his strongest argument for his system. Here I want to concentrate on one or two points that shall be concerning us in later chapters.

One small bit of background is needed before we look at the encounter with Wittgenstein. For reasons that I shall explain more fully in subsequent chapters, Katz takes the real target of Wittgenstein's philosophical critique to be Frege, and in this case specifically Frege's notion of the sense of a word—this may be thought of for the time being as its conceptual content: *cat* as "meaning" the idea of a furry animal that purrs—as a mode of determining reference (the way we use "cat" to refer to the real animal over there in the litter box). On Katz's view there is a great deal wrong with this notion of sense, but at the moment the crucial feature is that Frege's model assumes a one-way directionality in which sense *determines* reference: the word "cat" so to speak picks out things in the world that match up to its internal sense, and we would be misguided to use the word to refer to, say, trees or automobiles.

On Katz's interpretation of the type/token relation, by contrast, sense at the type level is merely something that *mediates* meaning or significance at the token level. In any actual speech act, in which various features of the extra-linguistic situation may be at work to determine meaning, the type-meaning of a word or sentence may be twisted, inverted, negated or otherwise deflected from its sense at the type level so as to take on various other kinds of significance. This is why Katz will always insist that an intensional semantic theory must be complemented by a strong pragmatic theory at the token level, the level at which utterances take on their full meaning in actual situations. (By *pragmatic* considerations I shall always mean *speech-act* considerations of the sort studied by Austin or Searle, or those featured in Grice's theory of conversational implicature. These are all the extra-linguistic conventions and circumstances which may allow the same utterance to function as a command in one situation, a promise in another, a warning in another, etc.)

Katz's point will be that, contrary to what some pragmatic theories imply—and Wittgenstein's doctrine of meaning-as-use denies altogether—type-meaning in this situation never gets wholly absorbed into the token or speech-act situation. The meaning given by the dictionary for *square*, for instance, is "a rectangle having four sides of equal length"; this is a good approximation of its type meaning in English, or what Katz will call its sense. But in fifties hipster slang the same word came to mean something quite different, something like "a person of old fashioned or extremely conventional taste." In the latter case, one obvious constraint on meaning is that the token must be used in some context where the literal use would be nonsensical (e.g., I am more likely to have this sense in mind if we are talking about my parents rather than trying to solve a geometry problem). But a second constraint, harder to see, is that the token-meaning continues to bear *some* relation to that literal meaning: our talk may be of parents, but a language of geometric figures and relations is always going to be governing what Katz will call the "pragmatic scatter" in any such situation.

Now in the "Slab!" example in *Philosophical Investigations*, as we shall see, Wittgenstein does want to argue that anything we could imagine as type-meaning—a sense belonging wholly to language as an abstract system of rules—can be shown, when we look carefully enough, to be absorbed entirely into the token or utterance situation. And Katz's riposte will be that Wittgenstein has failed to show what he thinks he has shown, and, more importantly, has neglected an entire dimension of language and meaning that simply can't be accounted for in terms of meaning-as-use. We will look at that example in a moment, but by way of seeing what the deeper issues are going to be, I want to look first at two moments in Katz's discussion of Wittgenstein that seem, on the face of it, more peripheral to the grand collision of the two systems.

They are not, viewed from one angle, peripheral at all. Through this whole section of *The Metaphysics of Meaning*, Katz is going to allow Wittgenstein to have his full say on various central issues of language and meaning, and is going then to point to some remainder that must be accounted for both by linguistic theory and philosophy of language. And always, the point will be roughly the same: Wittgenstein is going to be insisting in various ways that the central error of theorizing about such matters as language and meaning consists of looking for "invisible" entities, for "unseen" elements. Such theories go wrong, Wittgenstein says, by always imagining that they are looking for "something that lies *beneath* the surface. Something that lies within, which we see when we look *into* the thing, and which an analysis digs out. '*The essence is hidden from us*': this is the form our problem now assumes" (*PI* 92). Ultimately, of course, this will become the basis of Wittgenstein's epochal conception of philosophy as the source of its own problems, and of his own philosophical method as a kind of therapy that, as he says, "gives philosophy peace, so that it is no longer tormented by questions which bring *itself* in question" (*PI* 133).

This is the angle from which Wittgenstein will bring his own notion of meaning-as-use to bear on one of Frege's main ideas about propositions. Frege's notion was that sentences contain, besides their propositional content, an "invisible" element that allows them to function as statements, questions, and the like. Here again, the notion of propositional content is going to mean something like conceptual content. Frege thought that "It's raining outside" and "Is it raining outside?" expressed the same proposition—roughly speaking, what the sentence "says" about the state of affairs outside the window—but that the first had something like an assertive or assertoric force that allowed it to function as a statement ("It is the case that it is raining outside") while the second posits the same state of affairs but, additionally, wants to ask if it is the case. (In technical terms, the second sentence on Frege's view contains an interrogative or erotetic element in addition to the proposition.)

Now Katz is going to maintain that Frege was exactly right in his intuitions about these two sorts of sentence: there really is a proposition *and* an assertion in the indicative sentence, a proposition *and* a question in the interrogative sentence. (In syntactic terms, the subject-verb inversion that signals the shift from the indicative to the interrogative would make no sense if there weren't.) But in an age powerfully influenced by Wittgenstein's skepticism about meaning, and in particular by his relentless attack on the notion of "invisible" entities in language, this can no longer be taken as a matter of simple intuition. In the *Philosophical Investigations*, for instance, Wittgenstein used Frege's notion of an assertoric element to illustrate precisely what is wrong with metaphysical notions of language and meaning:

> Frege's idea . . . really rests on the possibility found in our language of writing every statement in the form: "It is asserted that such-and-such is the case."—But "that such-and-such is the case" is *not* a sentence in our language—so far it is not a *move* in the language-game. And if I write, not "It is asserted that . . . .", but "It is asserted: such-and-such is the case", the words "It is asserted" simply become superfluous. (*PI* 22)

Most readers of the *Philosophical Investigations* have taken this sort of analysis to be devastating in its anti-metaphysical implications:

Wittgenstein's examples in such cases are almost impossible to resist. It is true, as Katz notes, that one may sense a kind of question-begging tendency in Wittgenstein's remark that the phrase he adduces "is not a *move* in the language-game"—we have somehow already gotten, clearly, into a world here where meaning is somehow always going to come out as being equivalent to making a move in some language game, though at this early point this seems to be argument by assertion—but there need be nothing permanently disabling about that. Later arguments or analyses might make the point entirely plausible. So it is the simply the *superfluity* of "It is asserted that such-and-such is the case" that makes Wittgenstein's point here: everyone feels the redundancy, and redundancy seems in such cases always at least to suggest pointlessness, triviality, what is unnecessary or non-functioning.

What, then, about the other sort of syntactic form, the sort where, say, a subject–verb inversion is conventionally taken to signal an interrogative element? Wittgenstein's answer here is complex. He is not going to deny the interrogative or erotetic force of the inversion, but he is going to insist that such formal properties are as "neutral" as regards meaning-in-utterance as, say, the normal agreement of subject and verb in an English sentence. The formal properties are, so to speak, what make forms of utterance tools for our use, but only the use to which a form is put can ultimately determine what it "is" (what a mistaken metaphysics wants to talk about as the "meaning" of the utterance). And his example of how this happens is quite brilliant. Consider, says Wittgenstein, all the times we use interrogative sentences to make statements rather than ask questions, as when, meeting you at the bus stop and expecting no more than a conventional murmur of assent, I ask "Isn't the weather glorious today?"

The point Wittgenstein is making here is meant to have a sweeping implication. It isn't merely that one can use an interrogative sentence form to do something other than ask a question, but that the very notion of "form," which seems so strongly to invite us to think of the sentence as harboring an invisible erotetic force, is itself purely conventional. Thus, for instance, the shape of a hammer might seem to suggest that it is an object made for hitting nails, but if we think this we are without being aware of it actually letting our notion of a "standard" use impose on us something that derives from our form of life rather than anything about tools. It is not merely that what the hammer "is"—a paperweight, a doorstop, an *objet d'art*—can ultimately derive only from some use-within-a-context, but that apart from our conventions none of these uses has priority over any other.

Katz's rejoinder to Wittgenstein's example will be, interestingly, that it does not carry the concept of use far enough. For consider what must be true about any actual situation in which I use "Isn't the weather glorious today?" to make a statement about the weather. It must involve, at the very least, something resembling the sort of complex reflexivity that Grice means to account for in his notion of conversational implicature: it is not simply that the weather must be glorious, but that you must have already seen that is glorious, that I must see that you have seen this, that you must see that I have seen that you see this (etc). So it is that, having seen that I am using an interrogative form in a situation where it makes no sense to ask a question, you understand that I am making a conventional statement about the weather.

Katz's point will be that Wittgenstein has, contrary to his evident intention, constructed a case for the existence of an interrogative element. For, clearly, no such complex Gricean machinery would be necessary if there weren't something here that needed to be annulled or overridden. Given our normal conventions of speech, that something is overwhelmingly likely to be the erotetic force of the utterance. It is precisely because you see that a question is pointless in this situation, in short, that you hear me as making a statement. And even in the statement the erotetic sense lingers, which is precisely what gives meaning to the social convention: when I "ask" you about the weather, I invite you to join me in assent in a way that a simple pronouncement—"The weather is glorious today"—shuts out or forbids. A pragmatic theory taking Katz's intensional semantics as its point of departure might start here.

There is more. In Katz's New Intensionalism, as we shall see, a literal utterance is what occurs when sense at the type level coincides exactly with sense at the token level. When you and I are working on our geometry homework and I use *square*, the pragmatic or speech-act situation will suggest that what I most probably have in mind is, just as the dictionary says, a rectangle with four equal sides. Moreover, this will be what might be called the default position in any utterance situation. The sort of "pragmatic scatter" that occurs when extralinguistic constraints enter into the picture—as when, complaining about the extreme conventionality of my parents, I describe them as "square"—do so only in relation to the "ideal" possibility of a coincidence of sense at the type and token levels.

Usually, Katz will take the importance of this idea to be the way it permits a mapping of pragmatic scatter: a way of showing, as it were, which elements belong to the linguistic system and which to the speech-act situation. In the last chapter of this book I will suggest that this is its main significance for literary interpretation. In the case of Wittgenstein's "Isn't the weather glorious today?", however, it suggests a further point. We can very well imagine any number of situations in which Wittgenstein's example utterance actually *does* function as a question. Katz's example: we are taking a walk with a blind friend, and he gathers from the remarks of various passersby that the weather is glorious. Then we say something to suggest that the sky is, in fact, overcast and glowering. And our friend, honestly perplexed, asks "Isn't the weather glorious today?" The possibility of his *meaning* a question here is something that, on Katz's view, simply reverts to the prior possibility, which has so to speak been there all along, of a coincidence between type and token.

Wittgenstein's criticisms of Frege in this section of the *Philosophical Investigations* take much of their point from the famous thought-experiment Wittgenstein constructs to enable his readers to grasp the possibility of meaning as use. This is the imaginary stripped-down situation in which a builder orders his assistant to bring him items from separate piles of materials by uttering the term naming each item. Conceive of this, says Wittgenstein, as a complete primitive language. In the discussion that follows, the main role is played not by Wittgenstein but by his somewhat slow-witted interlocutor, who insists on hearing in the order "Slab!" a shortened or elliptical form of the command "Bring me a slab." In general terms, the interlocutor is all of us, not just philosophers who have deviated into nonsense by needlessly positing metaphysical entities but every user of ordinary language who has felt the power of language to bewitch the understanding. It is to free the interlocutor from such bewitchment that Wittgenstein will patiently ask questions and produce examples and analogies that seem to point to other, unthought-of possibilities—philosophy as therapy, once again, giving itself peace by freeing itself from its own entanglements.

As Katz notes, Wittgenstein has already been very clear about what sort of bewitchment or entanglement the analysis is supposed to resolve. The whole point of the shopping example with which the *Philosophical Investigations* begins is to show how error gets started in very ordinary situations. The shopper is to buy five apples. The storekeeper goes through various steps in which one sees that he is determining the meaning of *apple*, for instance, by reference to objects found in the apple drawer, and of *red* by matching the color of a red patch. And so, having been led by our identification with the shopper prematurely to commit ourselves to the notion that words mean by virtue of reference to objects, we try to think of a meaning for the word *five*. The point—bewitchment of the intellect by language par excellence—is that if we keep going in this direction we will soon be trying to think of "five" as an object, and then of numbers generally as objects, and so on into metaphysical never-never land. (Frege, whose influence on the early Wittgenstein was enormous, thought that mathematical objects really do exist, his intuition being that it would otherwise be nonsensical to talk about the truth or falsity of mathematical propositions.)

In the shopping example, Wittgenstein's response to this sort of incipient metaphysical lift-off is peremptory. It is that the "meaning" of *five* is just its role in shopping, the particular language-game in which it is involved. The interlocutor's voice is already a bit plaintive: "'But how does he know where and how he is to look up the word "red" and what he is to do with the word "five"?'—Well, I assume that he *acts* as I have described. Explanations come to an end somewhere.—But what is the meaning of the word 'five'?—No such thing was in question here, only how the word 'five' is used" (*PI* 1). As everyone who remembers reading the *Philosophical Investigations* for the first time will testify, the effect of this sort of endlessly patient untangling-of-the-web is exhilarating. It as though metaphysics were dissolving before one's eyes.

The point of the building-game in which the assistant answers the cry of "Slab!" by bringing a slab is to establish the notion of meaning-as-use at the earliest convenient moment. Once again, Katz notes, there is a kind of loading of the philosophical dice in imagining the building-game in the way Wittgenstein does. All that is going on is various forms of activity (building, ordering, bringing), and the language has been reduced to the simplest possible set of elements, so it is not hard to see that any notion of "meaning" is going to dissolve into some context of use here. Use is, so to speak, the only thing in sight. Nonetheless, there is nothing vicious about Wittgenstein's having set things up this way. If the point were, say, to establish the notion of meaning-as-use in the simplest possible terms before going on to more difficult cases, then the building-game would be serving an uncontroversial purpose. The first sign that Wittgenstein imagines it to be doing a great deal more than that comes, as I have noted, when the interlocutor keeps trying to insist that the utterance "Slab!" must be understood as a shortened version of "Bring me a slab!". The means through which Wittgenstein attempts to dispel this illusion are typically inventive:

> As far as the first question goes you can call "Slab!" a word and also a sentence; perhaps it could be appropriately called a 'degenerate sentence' (as one speaks of a degenerate hyperbola); in fact it *is* our 'elliptical' sentence.—But that is surely only a shortened form of the sentence "Bring me a slab", and there is no such sentence in example (2).—But why should I not on the contrary have called the sentence "Bring me a slab" a *lengthening* of the sentence "Slab!"?—Because if you shout "Slab!" you really mean: "Bring me a slab!".—But how do you do this: how do you *mean that* while you *say* "Slab!"? Do you say the unshortened sentence to yourself? (*PI* 19)

This is the moment at which Katz's New Intensionalism comes most violently into collision with the most powerful anti-intensionalist program in modern philosophy. Unfortunately for him, the arguments he must now use to make his case, though strong and compelling in their own terms, rest on a body of technical work in linguistic theory, which has tempted some readers to pass by the "Slab!" argument and proceed to Katz's more "accessible" arguments against philosophers like Quine and Davidson. Yet the technical details add up to a real intellectual drama here, in particular in the way the entire issue between Katz and Wittgenstein comes to turn on an otherwise innocent-sounding point of linguistic theory. This is the point that "Slab!", which Wittgenstein offers as a very parable of the sort of utterance that is erroneously imagined to signify by virtue of some unexpressed or invisible meaning hovering in the background—in this case, the interlocutor's unshortened "Bring me a slab!"—is not a genuine case of ellipsis. Wittgenstein has, no doubt without being aware of it, set things up in such a way that the doctrine of meaning-as-use cannot lose.

To look ahead just a bit, Katz will want in this situation to establish two points: (1) that Wittgenstein has based his most famous example of meaning-as-use on an elementary linguistic error, and (2) that when one has seen what the error is, one then *also* perceives the necessity of "theoretical" accounts of meaning—that is, precisely the sort of account that appeals to "invisible" or "unseen" entities to explain how words and sentences mean, that "looks beneath the surface" to explain what would otherwise remain inexplicable in our utterance. The key to Katz's position, in turn, is that his own semantic theory took as its original point of departure the Chomskyan revolution in theory of syntax, and such examples as Wittgenstein's "Slab!" make especially clear why such theoretical inferences as Chomsky's are necessary to account for what is actually at work *within* the system of grammatical rules governing any natural language.

Let us return for a moment to the puzzlement of Wittgenstein's interlocutor. He is clear enough about the rudiments of the language game he is being asked to contemplate, and he may even be perceptive enough to have glimpsed, at this point, the alternative possibility that Wittgenstein means his examples to suggest, that the meaning of "Slab!" in this situation is not in some longer version of the same sentence that hovers invisibly in the background, but just in the sum total of the activities (building, ordering, bringing) in which the builder and his assistant are engaged. Meaning comes from use, in short—from, more precisely, the entire complex set of rules and conventions and habits that make up "use" in any such situation—but because we inhabit this world of "use" as we inhabit our very consciousness, it has become invisible to us. So we look for "meanings" to explain something that needs no explanation.

With all this, the interlocutor keeps wanting to insist that there is something else going on here, that there *must* in some sense be an unelliptical form that explains how the builder is getting his utterance to work as a command. ("But when I call "Slab!", then what I want is, *that he should bring me a slab!*" [*PI* 20].) And what Katz is going to show, appealing to nothing more than a few simple rules of Chomskyan generative grammar, is that the interlocutor is quite right to think this. This is what we see, for instance, in the moment we set aside Wittgenstein's "Slab!" and look at the imperative forms more usually examined by linguists who want to account for elliptical syntax. Consider the following situation: a mother who knows that the family has to leave for a party in twenty minutes, and who suspects that her young daughter, a notorious dawdler, is dawdling again, comes into the child's room, points a finger, and says "Dress!"

The point of the generative grammarian in such cases will be that "Dress!" is the sort of thing an adequate syntactic theory must account for by positing ellipsis. To use the term favored by Chomsky in his earliest and most influential work, the utterance "Dress!" merely gives us the surface structure of the utterance. At the level of deep structure—that is, at precisely the "invisible" or "unseen" level that Wittgenstein wants to show is nonexistent—the imperative form contains an "unrealized" second-person subject. Moreover, this second-person subject is something that the daughter grasps when she understands that her mother has just issued an order. It is not part of the utterance, but neither, no matter how many Wittgensteinian hopes one might want to invest in details of the speech act situation (the mother's pointing finger, the hand on the hip, the glance at the watch), can it be understood as belonging to the extra-linguistic circumstances.

Moreover, the way in which Chomskyan theory demonstrates that there is an "invisible" second-person subject at the level of deep structure is to show by examples that denying its existence would in a sense involve throwing out our entire grammatical competence as English speakers. So, for instance, the linguist will show that any raising of the "invisible" subject to visibility only produces a sentence that any native speaker will accept as being identical in sense to the elliptical utterance: "You dress!", "You dress yourself!" "You dress yourself, you!" If, on the other hand, one tries to put a third-person subject in either pronoun position, one immediately "hears" that something has gone grammatically awry: *"Dress itself!", *"Dress themselves!", etc. (I observe the usual convention of putting an asterisk before ill-formed utterances.)

The magic of *"Dress itself!", it might be said, is that it allows one to "hear" the clash between the elliptical form of the utterance at the level of surface structure and the unrealized second-person subject at the invisible level of deep structure. This is the subject of the verb, in short, as it governs both utterance and comprehension but is nowhere present in the actual sounds made by the speaker. So to say that "Dress!" is an instance of genuine syntactic ellipsis is to say, in terms of Chomskyan theory, that the short form of the utterance has all along taken its sense from an unelliptical form beneath the surface:

$$((you)_{NP}((dress))_V(you+self)_{NP})_{VP})_S$$

The great problem with Wittgenstein's "Slab!", then, will be that it is not a verb but a noun. Nouns cannot take subjects, expressed or unexpressed. This is what makes Wittgenstein's choice of "Slab!", which would otherwise be no more than a minor linguistic mistake, into a philosophical error. He has staked a great deal of his relentless attack on "invisible" linguistic entities on a parable about language that will not bear the burden.

A number of important conclusions follow from this moment of local collapse in Wittgenstein's position. The first is that the interlocutor, who through so much of these early portions of the *Philosophical Investigations* has sounded hopelessly dim, here emerges as the unexpected hero of a victorious intuition. For in fact the interlocutor was *right* to keep insisting that "Slab!" must have meaning through its relation to some unexpressed longer sentence. He was wrong about "Slab!", of course, but that is only because Wittgenstein has unexpectedly installed a noun where one would normally find a verb in the imperative mood. But the interlocutor is not a linguistic theorist. What he has been trying to do, as an ordinary speaker of the language, is apply to Wittgenstein's "Slab!" the rules of inference that one more normally applies to such genuine cases of ellipsis as "Dress!", and as the examples adduced by Chomskyan linguists demonstrate, he was quite right to do so.

The second point that emerges from the "Slab!" encounter is that the notion of "invisible" or "unseen" entities assumes, in light of Wittgenstein's mistake, an altogether new significance. For as long as Wittgenstein was able to get us, along with his interlocutor, to keep seeing instances of "meaning" dissolve into contexts of use, the appeal to unseen entities always seemed to be metaphysics in the "bad" sense, a bewitchment of the intellect by language. But once one has seen that "Dress!" has an unrealized second-person subject, the invisible or unseen entities posited by Chomskyan syntactic theory become examples of *theoretical* entities, the equivalent in linguistic theory of atoms or molecules in physics or chemistry. That is, just as physics is given to positing an unseen dance of matter and energy in accounting for the tables and chairs of ordinary existence, an adequate theory of syntax (Chomsky) or semantics (Katz) will posit invisible entities like the "hidden" second-person subject of "Dress!" or the "unseen" senses *male* and *unmarried* as these are present in the decompositional sense structure of *bachelor*. This is no longer metaphysics in the Wittgensteinian "bad" sense, but simply and unremarkably what is called inference to the best explanation.

And last of all, Katz means to demonstrate through the "Slab!" example that redundancy, which Wittgenstein had been inviting us to see as a sign of nonsensicality in philosophical discussion, plays an indispensable role in the theoretical analysis of language. A statement, we remember Frege saying, contains both a proposition *and* the assertion of that proposition. And Wittgenstein's reply was meant as a knockdown: "if I write, not 'It is asserted that . . .', but 'It is asserted: such-and-such is the case', the words 'it is asserted' simply become superfluous" (*PI* 22). Thus began the Wittgensteinian disentanglement from metaphysics. But from a Chomskyan or Katzian point of view, what Wittgenstein has just done is to provide strong evidence that the statement *does* contain a assertoric element in addition to the proposition it makes: as with *you* in the case of "Dress!" or *unmarried* in the case of *bachelor*, the redundancy shows precisely that the element has been there all along. Contrary to his own assumptions, Wittgenstein is not exposing an absurdity but just being a good theorist of language.

Like Chomsky's generative grammar, Katz's intensional semantics posits a level where previously "unseen" entities are made suddenly visible by an adequate theory of language. In Katz's decompositional theory of sense structure, these invisible elements will be the *senses* contained within words considered as syntactic simples. The latter simply means that, when one is operating in purely formal terms of *syntactic* description, a singular noun like *bachelor* cannot be broken down into more elementary components. From the point of view of *semantic* theory, however, *bachelor* may immediately be seen to contain an entire structure of senses linked by relations of superordination and entailment. Thus, in commonsensical terms, our use of *bachelor* must, if we want to employ the word meaningfully, be understood to contain such senses as *human, adult, male, unmarried*, and so on.

Moreover, the system of entailments holding these senses in a fixed relation to one another will also be part of the word's sense, which is why, for instance, in the marker notation employed by Katz, *human* and *male* will be in a "superordinate" relation to *bachelor*.

Here lies the deeper significance of Katz's point about redundancy. In syntactic terms, the Chomskyan linguist who adduces *you* is simply using a syntactically redundant element to show that "Dress!" has a "hidden" second-person subject. Katz's intensional semantics will draw on redundancy in a closely related way, showing that, for instance, any competent speaker of English will "hear" redundancy in any case where a subordinate sense is raised to visibility at the utterance level. This is why, the theory of decompositional sense structure will tell us, *free gift* and *unmarried bachelor* and *female sister* are redundant when such similar phrases as *free ticket* and *unmarried graduate student* and *female applicant* are not. Here again, the redundancy that Wittgenstein used with such devastating effect against Frege may be seen simply as an indispensable means of bringing to light certain crucial pretheoretical intuitions about language.

It also brings to light an unexpected point about *a priori* truth. The *bachelor* example takes us to the very heart of Katz's New Intensionalism, semantic theory as it moves beyond the boundaries of linguistics to assume a very large burden of philosophical implication. For in such examples as *free gift* and *unmarried bachelor*, Katz came to realize at a certain point in his work on decompositional sense structure, we are dealing not only with linguistic redundancy but with what was once called necessary truth. As we shall see, this notion raises a huge number of logical and philosophical problems—Katz's New Intensionalism could in one aspect be described simply as a philosophical campaign to reinstate the idea of necessary truth implied by *unmarried bachelor*—but at an initial level the idea is simple enough: if it is true, a proposition like "All bachelors are unmarried" will be true in just the way that "$2+2=4$" is true.

To non-philosophers, this notion is likely to seem uncontroversial. The idea of logical or mathematical truth as something antecedent to or independent of our experience is very ancient, and still answers to a powerful intuition. To establish the truth of a proposition like "It's raining outside," we would want to say most of the time, one needs to check up on what is going on outside the window. In the case of

"$2+2=4$," it seems just as obvious that no checking up is needed, and even that the idea of checking up in such a case is not fully intelligible. Yet in contemporary philosophy, the same idea is controversial because it runs against the insistence of such major modern philosophers as Wittgenstein and Quine that necessary truth is itself an illusion. To a properly "naturalized" epistemology, to borrow Quine's famous phrase, logic and mathematics are simply very well-entrenched habits or practices, belonging to what Wittgenstein once calls "the natural history of human beings" (*PI* 415).

Yet this is, as Katz goes to some lengths to point out, a very recent development. For Locke, writing in the early period of modern philosophy, the notion of *a priori* truth exemplified in *All bachelors are unmarried* was so uncontroversial as to belong to the category of what he called "trifling propositions," which are what occur "when a part of the complex idea is predicated of the name of the whole" (qtd. in *Cogitations* 49). A generation later, Kant could say that such propositions, which he called analytical judgments, were true by virtue of expressing "nothing in the predicate but what has already been actually thought in the concept of the subject." And such truth was necessary truth. Given a proposition like *All bachelors are unmarried*, said Kant, "I have already in the concept . . . all the conditions required for my judgment. I have only to extract from it, in accordance with the principle of contradiction, the required predicate" (qtd. in *Cogitations* 53).

There are, Katz thinks, many reasons why this notion of analyticity no longer seems universally compelling, the most important being the turn to philosophical naturalism that has taken place in the hundred years or so since Darwin and Comte and J. S. Mill. But underlying that grand sweep of philosophical ideas there has all along lain, Katz wants to argue, a single persistent problem in logic that, because it has been thought to be irresolvable, has so to speak given naturalism free rein. This is the problem that, from Aristotle's *Organon* to Wittgenstein's *Tractatus* to the newest versions of the predicate calculus, logic has standardly been thought to concern relations of implication and entailment *only* as these hold among propositions. That is, from the syllogisms standardly taught to beginning students a century ago

All men are mortal.
Socrates is a man.
Therefore, Socrates is mortal.

to their counterparts in a modern logic course (Katz, *LOAO* 109)

> John is a bachelor
> Therefore, John is a bachelor or a bartender.

formal logic has had no way of handling the entailment relation that Locke and Kant thought was self-evidently exemplified in *John is a bachelor* $\longrightarrow$ *John is unmarried*. (The single exception in modern logic is Carnap's attempt to work out a system of "meaning postulates." As we shall see, Katz joins Quine, with whom he agrees on little else, in regarding this attempt as a complete failure.)

To look at the history of modern philosophy from this point of view, Katz argues, is to see that analytic entailment would become a kind of crossroads or parting of the ways in philosophical thought. For Kant, to whom *All bachelors are unmarried* is simply and uncontroversially an instance of *a priori* or necessary truth, there is no problem. And this will then remain the case with most of us who are not philosophers, and who realize that our world is in some irreducible sense held together by such entailments, as when we realize that *George had a nightmare* "necessarily" entails *George had a dream*, or when we are inclined to say that *Harry killed Sally* "logically implies" *Sally is dead*. And what we would tend to mean by this, if we knew the terminology, is that such entailments hold on the level of *a priori* or necessary truth.

For such twentieth-century philosophers as Wittgenstein and Quine, on the other hand, for whom an epoch in modern philosophy seemed to have begun with the work of Frege and Russell in symbolic logic, the absence of a means to account for entailments of the *All bachelors are unmarried* sort seemed to have shown that the very notion of *a priori* truth must be a mirage. Here lie the origins, on Katz's view, of Quine's famous attack on the analytic/synthetic distinction, as well as his various attempts to show that no coherent sense can be made of such notions as that of synonymy in linguistics. With Wittgenstein the story is somewhat different. The project of pursuing Russellian logical atomism to its limits in the *Tractatus*, Katz thinks, pressed home on Wittgenstein the degree to which analytic entailment lay permanently beyond or outside those limits. His response was the radical new method of the *Philosophical Investigations*, and the project of showing that even logic and mathematics are simply part of "the natural history of human beings."

The redundancy of *free gift* and *unmarried bachelor* thus provides the Archimedean point of Katz's New Intensionalism, which aims to carry through the Chomskyan revolution at the semantic level, and then to reinstate the notion of *a priori* truth much as it was understood by Kant and earlier philosophers. At the purely linguistic level, the crucial thing about *free* and *unmarried* as constituent senses of *gift* and *bachelor* will be, precisely, that they seem so strongly to insist on our positing the notion of senses as linguistic entities. For as Katz points out, the same sort of pretheoretical intuition that makes us want to hear *free* as a sense somehow "contained in" *gift* will also arise whenever we try to account for certain other linguistic facts—e.g., that *bank* is an ambiguous expression in English ("They caught the man who robbed the bank," "After taking a swim, I lay on the bank in the sun"), while *dust* is not only ambiguous but has antonymous senses ("While Susan dusted the living room, George went up in the Piper Cub and dusted the crops").

The trick here, Katz thinks, is simply to listen to the intuition that leads us to invoke senses in accounting for such facts. There is nothing obviously nonsensical, at any rate, about saying that *free gift* is redundant because *gift* seems to imply the sense of *free*, or that *bank* is ambiguous because in some utterances ("I'll meet you at the bank right after you're through swimming") it is impossible to know exactly which sense of the word is meant. At this level, Katz also thinks, one of the great advantages of ordinary intuition is precisely that it doesn't commit us to a theory. A great deal of philosophical ink has been spilled trying to show that senses are one thing rather than another— e.g., Frege on the Morning Star—or that they do not really exist. But a semantic theory aiming for explanatory adequacy will, on Katz's view, take no position at all at the outset: *senses*, whatever they turn out ultimately to be, are simply whatever properties and relations permit us intelligibly to say that *bank* is ambiguous as having more than one sense, that *dust* both has more than one sense and that these senses are antonymous, and so on.

The move from such ordinary observations to a notion of intensionality comes fairly early. As we have seen, the notion that senses are somehow "in" words comes up almost immediately when one is trying to explain why *free gift* is redundant. Here there is something like an exact parallel with Chomksyan generative grammar. Chomsky was led to posit the notion of deep structure when he saw that certain syntactically parallel expressions—the canonical examples are *John is eager to please* and *John is easy to please*—simply could not be accounted for on Bloomfieldian distributional or taxonomic principles. The syntactic relations that make *John* the subject in the first sentence and the object in the second hold, as it now became orthodox to say, beneath the surface level of such utterances. This is the spirit in which Katz will demonstrate that an ordinary word like *chair* is in fact composed of an entire system of senses and entailments—*Object (physical)* → *Furniture* → *[Etc]*—not directly visible in *chair* as a singular noun.

This is the theory of decompositional sense structure, and with it the notion of analytic entailment that, in Katz's view, has been the missing element in modern theories of logical implication. For on a purely commonsensical level, we want to say that such entailments as these are a constant and unremarkable element of linguistic meaning: to know that something is a *chair* must be to know that it is *furniture*, that it is a *physical object*, and so on. And we would be inclined to regard as logically contradictory—what Kant meant by saying that "the principle of contradiction" may be used to bring such senses to light—any such proposition as *The chair he smashed to bits was immaterial*. Yet the real power of this notion of implication will be, as we have seen, that it is able to show how a multitude of logical entailments may follow from a single or isolated proposition:

1) John is a bachelor, therefore
a) John is male.
b) John is adult.
c) John is unmarried.

Seeing the way in which *bachelor* yields such entailments, or the way in which *chair* implies *furniture* implies *physical object*, involves the system of representation associated with Katz's semantic markers, which play much the same role within his system as do P-markers, the branching tree-structures of the generative grammarian, within Chomskyan syntactic theory. We will look at examples of both in subsequent chapters. For the moment, however, the essential point is that Katz takes the system of entailments outlined above to permit a rigorous theoretical account of the phenomenon for which Kant, lacking either a theory or any system of formal representation, was compelled to account in merely psychological terms. To see that the *bachelor* must be *unmarried*, said Kant, is only to see that the predicate has been already thought as part of the subject. For Katz, it is to see that *unmarried* occupies a determinate place in the complex system of entailments of which the sense structure of *bachelor* is composed, and to see this is to see that "All bachelors are unmarried" is a necessary or *a priori* truth.

For all that it begins from a set of wholly ordinary intuitions about language, then—the redundancy of *free gift*, the ambiguity of *bank*, the antonymous senses of *dust*—Katz's New Intensionalism will end by insisting that decompositional sense structure represents a point of momentous intersection between language and logic, between the technicalities of formal representation in linguistics and such major philosophical problems as the theory of reference, the notion of necessary truth, and, ultimately, the existence of abstract objects. As I shall try to show, the notion of a world held together by entailments carried *within* language as a system of grammatical rules and relations, the idea of necessary or *a priori* truth as it works to sustain discourse even at the most ordinary level, possesses significant implications for literary theory.

I take the title of this chapter from W. V. Quine's essay "Epistemology Naturalized," in which he looks back on his own campaign against the concept of "meaning" in logic and linguistics. Quine's status as one of the two great naturalists of modern philosophy makes him one of the two anti-heroes of Katz's *The Metaphysics of Meaning*. The other, as we have seen, is Wittgenstein, whose naturalism proceeds from very different motives, but whose description of his own philosophy in *Philosophical Investigations* may in a general way be taken to illustrate the tendency of Quine's views as well: "What we are supplying are really remarks on the natural history of human beings; we are not contributing curiosities, however, but observations which no one has doubted, but which have escaped remark only because they are always before our eyes" (*PI* 415).

The view that Quine and Wittgenstein hold in common, for all the otherwise great differences in the way they do philosophy, is that the concept of "meaning" is the remnant of an exploded metaphysics, what Quine at one point calls a mysteriously meant entity called in to patch up deficiencies in philosophical reasoning. Again, the way Wittgenstein sums up the supposedly erroneous view is one Quine might very well accept as his own: "You say: the point isn't the word, but its meaning, and you think of the meaning as a thing of the same kind as the word, though also different from the word. Here the word, there the meaning" (*PI* 120). Quine has the same sort of thing in mind when he talks about meanings as having something of the same status as Homer's gods, or when he says that the study of meaning in linguistics strikes him as being in a state comparable to theology.

Wittgenstein's attack on the notion of meaning, and his attempt to show that everything that philosophy has tried to account for through an appeal to meanings really derives from language considered as part of "the natural history of human beings," is a version of the method we looked at in the last chapter, what Wittgenstein has in mind when he says that the philosopher's work is not to develop doctrines but to assemble reminders for a particular purpose. Quine's attack is more direct. Since his own interest is as much in logic as in language, and since the stronghold of "meaning" in logic is the idea of analytic truth, his attempt in "Two Dogmas of Empiricism" is to dispel the idea that propositions like "$2 + 2 = 4$" or "All bachelors are unmarried" have any special status in either logic or language. His assault, in short, hugely influential in contemporary philosophy, is on the very notion of *a priori* or necessary truth.

Quine's first move is against synonymy—i.e., the notion that "All bachelors are unmarried men" is analytically true because *bachelor* and *unmarried man* are synonyms. Quine's point is that this notion involves an invincible circularity. Consider. We say, "Surely 'bachelors are unmarried men' remains true in all circumstances because that is what one *means* by 'bachelor.'" To which Quine responds by asking what "means" signifies here. To which we respond by saying, if we are unwary, that "bachelor" is *defined* in the way we have said, as Quine would know if he would ask any native speaker of English or just check a good dictionary. To which Quine responds by asking—with, one is permitted to imagine, a spurious air of puzzlement—just what it is that leads native speakers and dictionary-makers to choose the definition "unmarried man" for "bachelor." To which we answer, perhaps a little less confidently now that we have glimpsed the problem, that the definition was chosen because it *means* the same thing as "bachelor, because the two are, um, synonyms." Whereupon Quine smiles.

This is Quine's central move against analyticity. A notion of analyticity based on definitions is caught in a vicious circularity because it resorts to an appeal to synonyms and synonymity deriving directly from the analyticity one was trying to explain in the first place. (Quine used a version of the same argument with devastating effect, as we shall see in chapter four, against Carnap's attempt to account for analyticity with a system of "meaning postulates.") The conclusion Quine then draws is this: since the notion of meaning as something "inside" language—that is, as a property of words and sentences—always seems to come down to some version of the synonymy argument, and since that argument is clearly circular, the place to go in search for the appearance of *a priori* or necessary truth in propositions like "All bachelors are unmarried men" is clearly *outside* language. That is, it must be a feature of the way words refer or otherwise relate to objects in the world: *bachelor* means, in short, by denoting a certain class of real human beings we call bachelors.

The way Quine attacks the notion of *a priori* truth in this case, though it bears less directly on our present concerns, is useful as suggesting what an *extensional* account of meaning looks like. For a pure extensionality would be something like the exact opposite of the intensionality for which Katz argues in *The Metaphysics of Meaning*. To see language in extensional terms is to say that words and sentences take on meaning entirely from the way they refer to extra-linguistic reality. (The term "extensionality" comes from a bit of technical jargon in logic: to say that "shoe" has a meaning by virtue of referring to the articles I am wearing on my feet is to say that these articles "fall under the extension" of *shoe*.) At an extreme, an extensional account of meaning would reduce language as such to nothing more than a system of signs themselves meaningless, the bursts of noise or marks on paper used to refer to physical objects like shoes.

Quine's view of language is something very like this, probably, Katz thinks, because he was writing under the influence of Bloomfieldian structuralism in linguistics, a theoretical model that really does, as we shall see, picture language as nothing more than an ordered system of meaningless sounds. On such a view, the notion that "All bachelors are unmarried men" is analytic means only that whenever you send me out to bring back ten bachelors, I will invariably bring back ten unmarried men. Yet it is not so far clear what logical harm is being done by the notion of analyticity here. It is true that we are no longer entitled to suppose that "unmarried" is somehow contained in the concept "bachelor," as Kant thought, but it is also true that whenever we are sent out to get bachelors we always bring back unmarried men. Why then, object to saying—Wittgenstein would, in fact, want to say something very like this—that my understanding that "bachelor" *means* "unmarried man" is just a perfectly sensible way of accounting for what I *do* when I am told to bring back a bachelor, or name the bachelors among my friends?

The logical harm being done in this situation, Quine argues, comes from the way it residually encourages an idea of *a priori* truth that will not survive a closer scrutiny. His example of why this is so is famous. Imagine, says Quine, a world in which every creature who has a heart *also* has kidneys. Then every time you send me out to bring back ten "creatures with hearts," I will return with ten creatures who also have kidneys. Yet the fact that this is invariably so cannot be due to anything about language or logic, as we might suppose if we began trying to construct some account of meaning that argued that "creature with a kidney" was somehow contained in the concept "creature with a heart," or that the latter somehow entailed the former "by definition." For truth here is coming not from "meaning," but certain facts about anatomy. On an extensional account, what we had been mistaking for analytic truths in such cases as "All bachelors are unmarried" are merely what are called coreferential expressions.

Quine's attack on analyticity was a major event in modern philosophy, his dismissal of *a priori* truth so decisive that no one was moved to ask, at the time, just why a purely extensionalist theory of meaning was felt to be so pressing a need. For if, indeed, the posit of meaning was like Homer's gods in the "bad" sense—in Quine's theory the posit of physical objects is also like Homer's gods, but in the "good" sense that it supports an empiricist epistemology—it is not clear that the notion needs a great deal of debunking. Like Zeus and Athena and Poseidon, we might suppose, the notion of meaning would fade to become nothing more than a remembered superstition. The same is even more true of "The Problem of Meaning in Linguistics," where Quine sets aside the issue of *a priori* truth in logic and mathematics to go after meaning as it has been assumed to be a property of words and sentences in natural languages.

The occasion of the urgency here, Katz thinks, is the philosophical reputation of Frege, who demands to be seen as the great blocking figure of philosophical naturalism in the twentieth century. For twentieth-century philosophy in a sense begins with Frege. Had it not been for his work in symbolic logic, especially as it laid the groundwork for the predicate calculus, there would have been no Russell and early Wittgenstein, neither the *Principia Mathematica* nor the *Tractatus Logico-Philosophicus* nor, subsequently, Quine's own work in logic. Yet Frege was an intensionalist. He thought that an account of meaning as internal to language was essential if one were to make coherent sense of certain important facts about denoting. In logic and mathematics, moreover, he was a Platonist who thought that logical and mathematical objects must be considered as having a real existence.

To understand why Quine was led to reassert a purely extensionalist account of language, it is necessary to recall the difficulties that led Frege to posit the notion of a sense internal to language—the *Sinn* of his famous distinction between *Sinn* and *Bedeutung*—in the first place. For extensionalist theories of meaning seem to ordinary intuition to have a great deal going for them. If you and I are shipwrecked on an island, neither speaking the other's language, it is very hard to imagine a situation in which I do not get you to understand what I mean by *tree* by first pointing at an object and then saying the word, repeating it with increasing emphasis until you have come to see that in my language "tree" refers to the leafy object with a trunk and branches that I point to when I utter the sound. And so on, presumably, to *rock* and *fish* and *mountain*, until we have gotten to at least a rudimentary bilinguality.

The extensionalist intuition in this situation is, in short, that the meaning of "tree" derives in direct terms from the object towards which I point, and this will then be true with such words as *table* and *chair* and *house* in more ordinary situations. This would give us, for instance, a nominalism like J. S. Mill's, for which the meaning of "table" just is the object in my dining room that I denote by uttering the word. Yet common nouns like *table* and *chair* present certain problems for extensionalist theory. What are we to say, for instance, is the meaning of "table" if the only table that has washed ashore on our island burns to ashes? But if we then say that that particular table only represented a "type" of object locally embodied in the table that burned, we seemed headed in the direction of a Platonism not easily countenanced by extensionalist theory. This is the sort of consideration that has given the theory of names its prominence in modern philosophy. For the one sort of noun that seems free from all such worries is precisely the proper name—*Paris, Boston, John, Susan*—which, by virtue of its relation to a unique individual, seems to avoid such problems.

Most extensionalist theories have seen no great difficulty about saying that the meaning of a proper noun, at least, just is the individual named by the noun. The meaning of "Paris" is the city in France picked out by that term, the meaning of "Reginald Witherspoon" is the individual it uniquely picks out—the only individual "falling under its extension"—in a given context. Russell actually does say this, in so many words. The problem that initially made Frege uneasy with the simple extensionalist notion of a name → object relation was, famously, that of identity. For language and logic involve free and frequent substitutions of terms. I may speak now of Samuel Johnson, now of the author of *Rasselas*, now of the subject of Boswell's biography. In this situation, it becomes essential to know which terms retain their identity with other terms, even for purely practical purposes. I may hire you to drop a water balloon on the President of the First National Bank, thinking this is still John Smith. But if Smith has gone on to another job, some other bank president is in for a nasty surprise.

This is the situation in which Frege took as his starting point Leibnitz's dictum that *Eadem sunt, quae sibi mutuo substitui possunt, salva veritate*: things are identical when one may be substituted for another while preserving the truth. There is a certain elegance to this concept: Johnson was the author of *Rasselas*, and Boswell's biographical subject, and he was also the individual called "Samuel Johnson," so nothing is lost by a free substitution of terms. Yet Frege, in an inaugural moment both of modern logic and analytic philosophy, saw a deep problem lurking here. For in logical terms, the only thing that an object can strictly speaking be said to be identical with is itself: you are you and not, even if you are an identical twin, someone else. (In logical terms, $a = a$.) But by the same token, to assert that $a = a$ doesn't seem to advance the discussion much. If you are wondering who John is, to be told that John is John leaves you more or less where you were.

As soon as one truly asserts that $a = b$, however, the logical and semantic situation alters dramatically. On the face of it, $a = b$ seems unproblematic enough: if the person his aunts call "Reginald" is called "Butch" by his playmates, then whenever Reginald is taking a shower Butch will be taking a shower too. Yet the assertion $a = a$ will be in every imaginable situation trivially and self-evidently true, and this is not the case, Frege saw, with $a = b$. To tell someone that Clark Kent is Clark Kent is to do only what Locke called trifling with words, as is telling them that Superman is Superman. To tell someone that Clark Kent is Superman may, however, come as a revelation. Frege's famous example was the planet Venus, which is both the Morning Star and the Evening Star. Here is a situation in which three terms take as their reference an identical object, and therefore ought on an extensionalist theory to have an identical meaning: Venus is Venus is Venus. Yet the assertion that Venus is both the Morning Star and the Evening Star is not self-evident in this way. On the contrary, it was an important discovery in astronomy.

The notion that expressions have objective senses apart from reference to objects is something that shows up especially well in what is called substitution into opaque contexts, which is what happens when, instead of asserting a proposition directly, I speak of it as something that is known, or believed, or thought, by someone else. Consider, said Frege, a proposition like "Galileo believed that the orbits of the planets were circles." Here the proposition "The orbits of the planets are circles" is false: as Kepler showed after a series of brilliant calculations, they are elliptical. Yet it is *true* that Galileo believed the planets had circular orbits. So Frege's proposition is true. And yet—the curious and important fact—though all propositions are equally false, Galileo did not believe in just any false proposition. He believed, specifically, in the state of affairs expressed in "the orbits of the planets are circles." Frege's own way of handling this was to set up a substitution procedure permitting what he called indirect reference, but the point that will be essential for understanding Katz's intensional semantics is that Galileo, in believing what he did believe, dwelt in a determinate world—the *specific* wrong version of reality, as one might way—expressed in a specific false proposition.

This notion of objective content is the basis of Frege's famous distinction between *Sinn* and *Bedeutung*, or sense and reference, and is the basis of his intensionalism. For in isolating the senses of "Morning Star" and "Evening Star," Frege brought into view a world that does not need, at this preliminary stage, to correspond to any external reality in order to be meaningful. Here, however, we encounter another problem. There is a tendency to think of any belief that exists in advance of reference or verification—or any belief that turns out to be simply false, such as Galileo's notion about planetary orbits—as being not a linguistic phenomenon but a subjective state, a merely mental or psychological phenomenon. Thus we might say that the four-year-old who on Christmas Eve says "Santa will visit tonight" simply has a false picture of the world, a neurophysiological brain state having to do somehow with chimneys and stockings and reindeer, and this neural state is, so far as it has any, the "content" of the statement about Santa.

Frege thought this view was wrong. Intensionalism in modern logic and linguistics begins in the way he demonstrated the point. For as "the Morning Star" and "the Evening Star" have different senses—i.e., objective linguistic content—so do statements. Thus Frege called "the orbits of the planets are circles" the *Gedanke* or propositional content of Galileo's belief about the planets. This is where the fact that even false propositions have a determinate content becomes crucial to the intensionalist position. For belief statements—in technical terms, statements expressing propositional attitudes—also have truth conditions. If I say "Galileo believed that the orbits of the planets were circles," I have just said something true. If, on the other hand, I say "Galileo believed that each of the planets was guided in its orbit by an angelic spirit," I have said something false. Yet each statement has *Galileo* believing something that is, so to speak, just as false as the other. The difference lies in their propositional content, and this, unlike belief, resists being reduced to a psychological state.

This is the line taken by Gilbert Ryle, whose account of propositions as abstract entities systematically developed Frege's insight. Thus Ryle pointed out, for instance, that I may make a given judgment ("It's raining") at widely different times, but the proposition towards which I adopt the attitude remains the same. By the same token, two or three different people may make the same judgement separately or independently, but *what* they make the judgement about remains identical. Or I may adopt quite different attitudes towards the same proposition ("Oh horrible, it's raining " [the family picnic is today]; "Oh marvelous, it's raining" [the crops have had none for weeks]) and yet the proposition remains identical. Or, finally, any proposition entertained by me now—"2 + 2 = 4," "it was raining on the morning of D-Day"—may be entertained by someone else a hundred years from now, and will be the same proposition.

Frege's notion of *Sinn* seems to put us pretty clearly on the path to a fully developed intensionalism, with sense or meaning conceived, as in Katz's New Intensionalism, in terms of relations and properties internal to language. How, then, given Frege's enormous influence on modern philosophy, was it possible for Quine only a few years later to argue with tremendous effect for a pure extensionalism, with *a priori* or necessary truth dismissed as an illusion and "meaning" itself pictured as a ghostly entity? Katz's answer is that Frege was not, for a number of reasons, in a position to follow out the implications of his own intensionalism. Instead, he reintroduced extensionalism at one remove by seeing *Sinn* as ultimately only a function of *Bedeutung*. In Frege's theory, in short, the sense of an expression like "the Morning Star" will always be seen as *a means of determining reference*.

Language thus hooks back up with the world, on Frege's account, by picking out that aspect of external reality caught by one or another sense. The intuition is the same as that behind extensionalist theories of meaning. One does look at the night sky, after all, to figure out things about Venus, and there is in this situation a powerful impulse to say that the world is determining meanings. The effect is to short-circuit Frege's intensionalism. We might very easily grant that, as Katz's New Intensionalism insists, the sense of *unmarried* is contained as a subordinate sense within *bachelor*, but this stops being important at just the moment we begin to worry about reference. For then we have no choice but to return to the domain of extensionality. If you have ordered me to round up and bring down to the station house all the bachelors at the party, my best move is clearly to start checking marital records rather than undertaking a semantic analysis of the word.

The real legacy of Frege's theory of meaning to modern philosophy, in Katz's view, is the "mixed" notion of sense as determining reference, which he sees as having remained a source of puzzlement even in contemporary philosophy. The best example, perhaps, is the description theory of names, which goes back to Russell's notion of definite descriptions. The theory begins in the observation that a person may be described in various ways, as, for instance, the starting shortstop for the New York Yankees, or the father of two children named Rachel and Roscoe, or the owner of the new Porsche in the parking lot. The point is then that names and definite descriptions seem to be freely interchangeable in all sorts of circumstances. If Ralph Roe is the Yankee shortstop, saying "I didn't think the shortstop was a very good fielder," insofar as it seems to be propositionally identical to "I didn't think Ralph Roe was a very good fielder," seems to be, exactly as Frege thought, a way of determining reference through sense.

The intuitive appeal of this notion increases as soon as we imagine a situation in which there are multiple bearers of a single name. So, for instance, I ask you to deliver an urgent message to John Smith, and you point out that there are ten John Smiths in the building. This is precisely when a multiplication of descriptions—I want the John Smith who was born in Maine, the one who graduated from Yale, the one who has a birthmark shaped like a clover on the inside of his right ankle—seems most clearly to hold out the promise of catching a unique "John Smith" in the network of descriptions. Here we seem to be moving towards something very much like an intensionalist theory of naming, exactly the sort of thing Frege was aiming for with the notion of *Sinn* in the case of "the Morning Star" and "the Evening Star." And it seems equally clear that some sort of intensionalist theory is needed: since any one of the ten John Smiths falls under the extension of the simple name "John Smith," pure extensionality pretty obviously fails to do the trick.

Yet the notion of sense as a means of determining reference leaves the description theory of names with serious problems. Consider, for instance—I borrow loosely from Kripke, to whom we shall turn in a moment, and who is himself borrowing from Frege—the network of descriptions we might use in trying to make sure that our use of the name "Aristotle" referred to the Greek philosopher. Since many Greeks at the time and subsequently have been named Aristotle, we clearly need something like a net of definite descriptions. But this doesn't seem to present any great difficulty. We want, we might imagine ourselves saying, the Aristotle who was tutor to Alexander, or the Aristotle who wrote the *Nicomachean Ethics*, or the Aristotle who was Plato's pupil. All of these taken together seem to converge on the name "Aristotle" as this then picks out a unique individual alive during a certain historical moment in ancient Greece.

As Saul Kripke so powerfully demonstrated in *Naming and Necessity*, however, combining an alternative notion of naming originated by Ruth Marcus with his own inventive use of counterfactuals, the theory can't be made to work. For it is entirely possible, Kripke points out, that evidence might turn up tomorrow that someone else, and not Aristotle, was the tutor of Alexander the Great. In this case we should not want to say that there had been anything wrong with our use of "Aristotle," only that we had gotten one of the facts about him wrong. But then this will also be true if the *Nicomachean Ethics* turns out to have been written by someone other than Aristotle. Rather than doubt that there was an Aristotle, we should simply deduct it mentally from the corpus of his known works. But then—Kripke's argument works relentlessly—we could have *every* description we had associated with "Aristotle" proven wrong, and it is wholly conceivable that the individual we have always referred to by that name existed and was so called.

The meaning of names like "Aristotle," then, must lie elsewhere than in descriptions, senses, propositions, and the like. Kripke's solution is to adopt J. S. Mill's position on names, which is that they have no sense. The meaning of a name just is the object it denotes. It operates, to use Kripke's terminology, as a rigid designator. And a name *gets* its meaning from what Kripke calls a baptismal event. (The baptismal naming of human babies, though it functions nicely to show how "John Smith" or "Reginald Witherspoon" get hooked up with their bearers, is merely a local and literal example of what Kripke has in mind. Paris and the Pan Am building get their names in the same way.) After the baptismal event, the only requirement is that my use of "John Smith" or "Paris" demonstrate a continuity with earlier uses, thus reaching back in time to the "baptism" through which the name was linked with its bearer.

This is extensionalist theory at its most creative. It works brilliantly against Fregean intensionalism, and does so by exposing the problems involved in any version of Frege's notion of sense as a means of determining reference. For Katz, furthermore, Kripke's attack on the description theory of names may be taken as an epitome of anti-intensionalist arguments in twentieth-century philosophy. All have been narrowly targeted at the Fregean notion of sense, and all have assumed that, when that notion of sense is exploded, the only remaining alternative must be an extensionalist account of meaning. Katz's rejoinder will be that his own New Intensionalism remains untouched by such arguments as those of Quine and Kripke, partly because it is altogether more radical in the way it posits sense as an internal feature of language, and partly because it comes backed by a linguistic theory that was unavailable when Frege was giving his account of *Sinn* and *Bedeutung*.

In the meantime, Katz sees unresolved problems lurking for Kripke's theory of names. They are precisely the sort of problem that, on his view, suggests why an intensional account of meaning remains indispensable even when one has gotten rid of a great number of difficulties by appealing to baptismal events and rigid designators. What is one to do, for instance, in the case of "names without bearers"—I put the phrase in quotes because this is the title of Katz's classic paper on the subject—or of names with multiple bearers? The first is the problem of the child who thinks Santa Claus is coming tonight, and who moreover says this (states it as a proposition) as she is drifting off to sleep on Christmas Eve. The other is the problem of ten people in the building all of whom bear the name "John Smith." In the latter case, since Kripke has said that the meaning of a name (after baptism) is its bearer, and since there are now ten bearers, Kripke either has to say that we are dealing with a single name with ten meanings or, on the contrary, ten different names.

As it happens, Kripke takes the latter way out, claiming that "John Smith" operates in this case something like a homonym, with phonetic identity from case to case disguising the fact that ten quite different names are involved. (He also suggests, quite unusually for Kripke, that a proper notation—e.g., Smith$_1$, Smith$_2$, Smith$_3$ . . .—would make the logical and semantic reality clear.) Katz has an analysis that, as we shall see in a moment, handles this sort of example very elegantly, but his initial interest in raising the problem is less in the technical details than in inducing the strain that comes from taking a pure extensionalism to its limits even when the result is strongly counterintuitive. His point here is that two John Smiths who meet and say "We have the same name" are not claiming a mere homonymic identity between what are really two different names. They are saying they have the same name.

The alternative theory of names proposed by Katz is highly original. He argues that (1) proper names in a language have senses in advance of reference, as do common nouns, but (2) the sense of a proper name incorporates into itself a use-mention distinction restricting candidates in any pragmatic context to bearers of the name mentioned, while (3) incorporating as well an anaphoric requirement that holds together the name-bearer relationship in purely grammatical and logical terms before any *token* of the name is used in actual speech or discourse. (An anaphor is an element that is referentially dependent on another in the same construction, as a pronoun "refers back" to its antecedent, or, less standardly, may "refer ahead": "If *she* comes while I'm still in the shower, tell *Susan* to wait for me.") On Katz's theory of naming proper names have a sense (meaning or significance wholly internal to language) that looks like this: "The thing which is a bearer of 'N'" (NWB 5).

This formulation, understood in relation to the rest of Katz's theory, is very powerful, with every element—the definite article *the* before "thing," the indefinite *a* before "bearer," the quotation marks around N to hold constant a certain use-mention distinction—doing a great deal of logical and semantic work. What it permits is nothing less than a metalinguistic requirement—a set of constraints on the way a linguistic element must be used in any context outside of language—that, so to speak, remains within the language as a purely semantic principle. What allows it to do so is the type-token distinction discussed in chapter 2. For proper names are now among the expression types with a power to impose themselves in certain ways—but not, as we shall see, in others—on their tokens as used in actual speech or writing. In the more specific terms of Katz's account of names, this gives us "John Smith" as a type—wholly meaningful in the language *as* a name before ever being used—tokens of which may be used in any number of situations to refer to actual individuals.

The constraints on use in the token context are simply those captured in Katz's formulation of sense as a metalinguistic principle: anaphor and preservation of the use-mention relation. This gives names in Katz's theory a function somewhat similar to pronouns as we tend ordinarily to account for their use. The term *this*, for instance, exists in the language as a type in just the sense meant by Peirce: before its twenty occurrences on this page, or in my conversation with you, it belongs to a pure realm of rule-governed possibility, language as it so to speak exists apart from any world where pronouns are actually used. But then an adult at a garden party holds up an object to a crowd of children and says "I want each of you to bring me a flower like *this* [holding up a yellow tea rose]" and the word has succeeded in referring—more precisely, one of its tokens has—in a way that does not somehow demand that we get gardens or flowers into its semantic content.

The way description now enters the picture nicely illustrates, on Katz's view, the degree to which Russell's description theory of names was nothing more than an elaboration of Frege's mistaken concept of sense. For if a token of the type "John Smith" is ambiguous or unclear in a pragmatic context, description will now flow in as reference-fixing amplification: "No, I mean you should give it to the John Smith who's drinking the gin tonic," or "who is married to Jane," or whatever. A child at the garden party too short to see the speaker might similarly depend on a taller child for instructions: "It's a yellow flower. It has thorns on its stem," etc. It is at this point that we are in a position to see that the whole problem with Frege's account was that it prematurely tried to force merely contingent aspects of the world—the gin tonic that John Smith is drinking when he might just as well have been Reginald Witherspoon drinking bourbon—into language, which, as a system of purely syntactic and semantic rules, has no place for them.

The power of Katz's New Intensionalism may be seen, I think, in his final move against Kripke on the subject of naming. For the other embarrassment of Kripke's theory, on which names are merely bursts of meaningless noise until the baptismal event that links them with a bearer, is that names like "Santa Claus" must then actually be treated as noise. This is in fact exactly what Kripke, pushed to the wall on this particular problem, does. "Santa Claus" means in the same way as "Bandersnatch" (from Lewis Carroll's nonsense poem *Jabberwocky*): it is given a kind of specious stability by being associated with a fixed referential context, but it is in semantic terms simply empty. But then, as Katz observes, we are left with no way of accounting for an important fact: a child who has grown old enough to be told that there is no Santa Claus is being given a significant piece of information. Kripke's last move in this situation is to try to reformulate the nonexistence of Santa Claus in terms of propositions and truth conditions. Katz's counterargument, to which his theory of names without bearers fully entitles him, is that children who believe in Santa Claus believe not in propositions about Santa Claus but in Santa Claus.

There remains the question of why such philosophers as Quine and Wittgenstein, in rejecting Frege's notion of sense, then turned to naturalism, and specifically to a view of language as an evolved system of conventions not essentially different from marriage customs or tribal dances. The answer is, Katz thinks, partly that there was no really powerful linguistic theory in existence at the time Frege was constructing his account of *Sinn* and *Bedeutung*, so that language had begun to look, as it were by default, like just one "naturally evolved" human practice among others. This is the situation that Katz sees as having been changed in a radical way, as we shall see in the next chapter, by the

Chomskyan revolution in linguistics. But beyond that, Katz thinks, there is the problem that Frege's own work in symbolic logic, and its enormous subsequent influence on philosophers from Russell to Quine, mandated what he calls a *Begriffsschrift* conception of language.

The word *Begriffsschrift* comes from the title of one of Frege's best-known writings, in which he sketches a conceptual notation or "logically perfect language" that might serve as an alternative to ordinary language, with its imprecision, ambiguity, and general fuzziness about logically significant relations. In a sense, the modern student who learns *Principia* notation in an introductory logic course is learning *Begriffsschrift* as Frege meant the term, but Frege's real point had less to do with notation than with a sense of underlying logical form that, at the time he was writing, was still new enough to seem revelatory. Consider, to take a famous example, Russell's problem about the King of France. We have no problem, if we know from experience that our mother's brother has lost all his hair, with propositions like

    1) Uncle Harry is bald.

But at a time when, the monarchy having been abolished, there is no King of France, there seems to be a problem about such propositions as

    2) The present King of France is bald.

Since both sentences are perfectly grammatical, however, the problem is not in any evident sense linguistic. It seems to be a problem about the logic of propositions.

This is the problem Russell resolved by introducing the existential quantifier ($\exists$), which today is also taught in every introductory logic course. Russell's answer to the problem was to say that "Uncle Harry is bald" contains *two* propositions, namely, that (1) there is such a person (Uncle Harry), and (2) that this person is bald. (I set aside a third proposition—"There is only one such person"—as inessential to the point I'm trying to bring out.) This is what is symbolized in the notation, where the *x* is "Uncle Harry," "B" is the predicate "is bald," and $\exists$ claims the existence of *x*: "There exists an *x* such that *x* is Uncle Harry and *x* is bald." The point of a logical notation is then to permit one to see that "The present King of France is bald" works in exactly the same way, namely

    $\exists x (Kx \& Bx)$

Thus the puzzle is solved. "Uncle Harry is bald" is true or false, if it is so, in straightforward terms: his baldness is something we can check up on by asking Uncle Harry to send a recent picture. But "the present King of France is bald" is misleading because the part of the proposition symbolized by $\exists x \, (Kx)$ is not satisfied: there is no present King of France, and so questions about his baldness are, Russell thought, in a certain way meaningless.

To get the point of Frege's *Begriffsschrift*, it is necessary only to see how symbolic notation in such cases encourages the notion that one is looking "into" language to perceive something like underlying logical form. Katz also thinks that it is important to stress, if we want to understand why philosophers like Quine and Wittgenstein then resort to linguistic naturalism, the way in which the same *Begriffsschrift* perspective encourages a notion of language as the product of evolutionary forces, more like the human eye or hand, than a formal system like logic or mathematics. This seems to be what Frege himself had in mind when he drew an analogy between the relation of his own logical notation to ordinary language and the relation of the microscope to the eye: "Viewed as an optical instrument, says Frege, the human eye "reveals many imperfections, which usually remain unnoticed only because of its intimate connection with mental life. But as soon as scientific purposes place strong requirements upon sharpness of resolution, the eye proves to be inadequate" (qtd. in *LOAO* 162).

In this situation, the impulse to leave ordinary language behind in favor of the world of lucid logical relations mirrored in the *Begriffsschrift* will be very strong. It is the impulse that, in modern philosophy, leads from Russell's *Principia* to Quine's *Mathematical Logic* to Kripke's work in modal logic. But then, having left ordinary language behind, one will also have left behind various forms of entailment and implication that cannot be handled in the *Begriffsschrift*. A classic example is the sort of analytic entailment represented by "All bachelors are unmarried." This is where the turn to linguistic naturalism tries to solve an enormous problem by making it possible to declare that, in effect, the problem does not exist: the analyticity of "All bachelors are unmarried" is simply illusory, the notion of sense or meaning on which it depends a folk superstition deriving from an unexamined use of ordinary language.

This, or something very like it, is Quine's move in "Two Dogmas" and "The Problem of Meaning in Linguistics." One is to solve the problem of meaning, much as behaviorism solved the problem of the mental, by demonstrating that on a properly rigorous view it does not exist. With Wittgenstein the case is more complicated, and more instructive for an understanding of Katz's New Intensionalism. For the Wittgenstein of the *Tractatus*, Katz thinks, went further in the direction of a *Begriffsschrift* conception of language than anyone in previous philosophy, and when he had seen that certain formal problems remained wholly irresolvable, his conclusion was that the entire way of thinking about logic and language represented by a *Begriffsschrift* conception must be wrong. Upon further reflection, Katz also thinks, his own *Tractatus* would come to represent for Wittgenstein the terrible mistake that begins in thinking that "the *essence* of language, of propositions, of thought," is "something that lies *beneath* the surface. Something that lies within, which we see when we look *into* the thing, and which an analysis digs out" (*PI* 92).

This opens a clear path to the *Philosophical Investigations*, and to the method that, as we have seen, works to dissolve the metaphysics that Wittgenstein thought language produces by an entanglement in its own rules. The method will consist, to borrow Wittgenstein's phrase one last time, of "remarks on the natural history of human beings," and its naturalized view of language—of use, of habit, of language games and forms of life as the source of "meaning"—remains the most compelling version ever developed. Our business from this point on will be with the way Katz, in the name of the Chomskyan revolution in linguistics, will counter such views with his own New Intensionalism. Before we altogether leave Wittgenstein and the *Begriffsschrift* conception of meaning, however, I want to look at one last example that may serve as a reference point for later discussion.

The example comes from Wittgenstein's *Tractatus*, specifically the point at which he is puzzling over the way in which certain propositions seem to exclude each other even though logic provides no account of the way in which they do so. For Wittgenstein, what is at issue is an increasingly urgent awareness that a certain kind of necessary truth cannot be handled within the scheme developed in the *Tractatus*, either at the technical level of the logical calculus and atomic propositions or the more overtly philosophical level of the picture theory of language. The problem is necessary truth as it seems to be involved in a common kind of contradiction. I point, let us say, to a blue object and announce that it is "blue all over." And you, standing beside me in good light with normal color vision, announce that, to the contrary, it is "red all over." The two propositions, we want to say, contradict each other, but how?

There is a deep problem here. The way in which Wittgenstein initially tried to solve it was by appealing to an idea of negation in some sense authorized by the picture theory: a proposition asserts that p, such that $\sim p$ becomes not simply an erasure of p but a denial that *that* state of affairs exists. (The symbol p stands for any proposition: "The object is red all over." The negation sign simply asserts that p is false: "It is not the case that the object is red all over.") Wittgenstein is supposed to have gotten the picture theory from seeing a model used in a court case about a traffic accident: a table-top model of streets and buildings, tiny cars and trucks representing the actual vehicles. One can at least conceive of "positive negation" as working like this: a defense counsel duplicates a certain sequence of events using the model then turns to the jury and says "Now that is exactly what did *not* happen."

In some ways, the way Wittgenstein explains this notion in the *Tractatus* bears a resemblance to Katz's account of the role played in negation by decompositional sense structure, though there are also important differences. Here is Wittgenstein:

> One could say, the denial is already related to the logical place determined by the proposition that is denied.
> The denying proposition determines a logical place *other* than does the proposition denied.
> The denying proposition determines this logical place, with the help of the logical place of the proposition denied, saying that it lies outside the latter place. (qtd. in мм 68)

This is ingenious, and moreover seems to have something intuitively plausible about it. We do intuitively feel that a denial of the proposition "It's raining" is not just what might be called a cancellation or erasure of the original proposition, but obliquely a claim that the weather must be doing something else. Yet it leaves the *Tractatus* with an irresolvable problem. For Wittgenstein's whole point in the *Tractatus* has been that nothing exists in language except logical truths and elementary propositions, and logical truths are by nature empty or tautologous. So the problem becomes that the *Tractatus* permits as negation only the external operation symbolized by "~". The crucial point is that the dilemma here is the dilemma of logic as such, as pertinent to Quine's specification of a logical language in "Two Dogmas" (*LPV* 30) as to Wittgenstein's logical atomism in the *Tractatus*. It is that there is no account available of the sort of unactualized or unformalized negation that seems to be occurring when you stand beside me and insist that the object I declared to be blue is actually red. (I shall from this point on use a shorthand: "the object is blue" means "the object is *completely* blue," etc.) Wittgenstein at one point tries to get around this with speculation about "the logical structure of color":

> For two colors, e.g., to be at one place in the visual field, is impossible, logically impossible, for it is excluded by the logical structure of color. . . .
>
> (It is clear that the logical product of two elementary propositions can neither be a tautology nor a contradiction. The assertion that a point in the visual field has two different colors at the same time, is a contradiction.) (qtd. in *MM* 69)

The last sentence, as Katz points out, gives the essence of the problem, but does nothing to solve it. For on the *Tractatus* scheme any proposition p and any proposition q simply yield an ordinary conjunction, as when "the object is spherical" and "the object is red" comes out uncontroversially as "the object is spherical and the object is red" ($p\&q$). Yet "the object is blue" and "the object is red," are also atomic propositions. So now $p\&q$ gives us "the object is blue and the object is red," which *is* controversial. For such propositions seem in some very powerful but as-yet-unanalyzed way to exclude each other, but there is nothing in the formal representation to suggest why this should be so. Wittgenstein returned to this problem, Katz points out, in the one paper he ever published after the *Tractatus*, but with no greater result than to remark unhelpfully that "Atomic propositions, though they cannot contradict, may exclude each other" (qtd. in *MM* 69).

For Wittgenstein, the irresolvability of such problems would come to suggest that there must be something deeply wrong with the way they were posed. His own puzzlement would later seem to him an allegory of philosophy as the source of its own entanglements in metaphysics. For Katz, however, the moral of the story will be that what is needed is a way of dealing with entailment, contradiction, and *a priori* truth that has been unavailable in standard logic, and that only becomes available through an account of decompositional sense structure. We shall see in chapter five how he solves Wittgenstein's problem about color and logical contradiction. Until then we may take his point as being that the intuition of necessary truth in such cases is extremely powerful—if an object is red all over, we want to say, it simply *cannot* be blue all over—and that what is needed, rather than a philosophical naturalism that conjures the problem away in the name of "metaphysics," is a linguistic theory that covers the missing ground.

Although Quine has never been a nominalist as such—he has always countenanced sets and universals—his impatience with the notion of meaning in such essays as "The Problem of Meaning in Linguistics" may be seen to derive from a nominalist view of language. In general terms, this is *nominalism* much as the medieval philosophers understood it: the idea that only individual or particular entities exist, and that any higher-order abstraction used to refer to them will be a mere *nomen* or name, an empty sound signifying nothing. Thus the word *cat* has meaning, on a nominalist account, so long as I use it to refer to this or that furry entity that may be prowling my back yard looking for chipmunks. But as soon as I start thinking that there must be some more general quality of "catness" shared by these entities—or, more precisely, that *cat* somehow really takes such a quality as its object of reference—I am headed for what a Wittgensteinian would call the bewitchment of my own intellect by language.

One of Katz's major claims will be that his New Intensionalism in a certain sense carries through the Chomskyan revolution in linguistics, and by way of seeing why Chomsky's theory has been considered revolutionary it is useful to try to imagine what a pure nominalism in the study of language would look like. This would not be a nominalism that stayed at the relatively high order of generality at which Quine contests the notion of "language-independent meanings," but a version that reached all the way down to the level of phonology, morphology, and the most basic categories of syntax. For in the study of language even the most ordinary terms—"phoneme," "vowel," "consonant," "syllable," "word," "noun," "verb," etc.—are higher-order abstractions. Anyone who studies language, clearly, is going to have to use some of these terms. It is the *way* they are used that makes one a nominalist, or not, in linguistics.

The view that is wanted begins, at least, from a notion of language as brute noise. It is not an easy view to grasp, because even in situations where we do not understand a language we seldom hear it as noise. If I am in Tokyo and overhear a couple at the next table talking in rapid Japanese, my tendency is to say, not that they are making noises at each other, but that they are speaking a language I don't understand. Richard Feynman is said to have invented a non-existent language that consisted of meaningless sounds that so perfectly imitated the intonational patterns of Italian—it included frequent -*a* and -*o* endings—that it was able to fool everyone except Italians. Perhaps that would qualify as an example of "nominalist language" in the sense of language as pure sound or noise, though even there the intonations, which a linguist would want to describe in terms of supersegmentals, and the endings, which are a kind of mock-morphology, introduce a problematic element.

The point of the exercise is that it takes us back to what linguistics was doing, or thought it was doing, in the period before Chomsky wrote *Syntactic Structures*. Due to the enormous prestige of Leonard Bloomfield, the dominant model was a taxonomic grammar that, in the name of a properly "scientific" approach, imagined itself to be studying language as a system of sounds or scratchings that were, first and foremost, physical events. Non-linguists, Bloomfield said, with evident disdain for those who suppose otherwise, "constantly forget that a speaker is making noise, and credit him, instead, with the possession of impalpable 'ideas.' It remains for linguists to show, in detail, that the speaker has no 'ideas', and that the noise is sufficient." Language can be objectively studied (that is, studied "as part of nature") wrote Zelig Harris, Chomsky's own teacher, only if one "considers speech and writing not as expression of the speaker which has particular, introspectively recognized, meanings to the hearer, but rather as a set of events—sound waves or ink marks" (qtd. in *LOAO* 25).

This account of language harmonizes readily with a philosophical naturalism like Quine's, and Katz will point out with great effect that, at the time Quine wrote "The Problem of Meaning," the Bloomfield-Harris model was the only one available to him. For an essential point about taxonomic grammar is that it requires a rigorously nominalistic view of language. One has the sound waves or ink marks—Harris's "events"—and a few observed regularities, and that is all. Consider, for instance, the well-known paper by Jean Berko in which a group of small children is shown a picture of an imaginary animal called a Wug. Shown a picture with two such animals, the children unhesitatingly identify them as Wugs. For the taxonomic grammarian the -s marking the "normal" distinction between singular and plural was the beginning and end of the story.

For Chomsky, whose revolution would be carried out in the name of explaining language acquisition, the same story is one in which rule-mastery is proceeding at a very nearly miraculous rate, so that the children are, from degenerate data—the ums and ers and sentence fragments of ordinary speech—and a very small sample of utterances, internalizing a total system of rules that will shortly allow them to utter wholly grammatical sentences never before uttered in the language. Though Katz will for good reasons go to some length to show why Chomsky's focus on acquisition—his nativism, or conceptualism, or competencism, as it is variously called by Katz and others—leads ultimately to an impoverished account of language and meaning, one sees immediately why it worked so conclusively against Bloomfieldian taxonomy. As Chomsky himself demonstrated in *Aspects of the Theory of Syntax*, a purely inductive or "bottom up" approach cannot even construct the categories needed to represent grammatical rules.

The attempt to imagine language as a mere system of regularized noise, moreover, involves a certain mental strain, which is doubtless why there is very often a strong sense of repressed linguistic intuition in the work of the taxonomic grammarians. One sees this most clearly, perhaps, in the case of substitution procedure. The distributional methods originally employed in taxonomic grammar retain an honorable if minor role in modern linguistic theory. To view them in operation is to see readily enough why, even within the nominalist universe of Bloomfield or Harris, they must at times have seemed to be pointing insistently beyond mere regularities to a more complex level of linguistic reality. Consider, for instance, a standard test for whether a verb is modal. If there is a question, one simply substitutes the verb into the frame sentence

_____ I be frank?

(Since we are about to cover a good deal of Chomskyan ground, I should perhaps remind the reader of the convention that an asterisk signals an ill-formed or "ungrammatical" expression.) The results will look like this:

(a) *Must/Can/Could/Shall/Should* I be frank? [Modal]
(b) **Walk/*Attempted/*Am/*Protested* I be frank? [non-modal Verb]
(c) **Small/*Pretty/*Intelligent/*Round* I be frank? [Adjective]
(d) Etc.

Or consider the substitution rule based on the grammatical principle that only Adjectives and Adverbs can occur after *very*:

(a) He is very *intelligent* [very + Adj]
(b) He argues very *intelligently* [very + Adv]
(c) *She very *enjoys* water skiing [very + Verb]
(d) *Very *professors* enjoy reading Frege [very + Noun]
(e) *He walked very *up* the slope [very + Preposition]

Even the most ordinary substitution procedures, in short, seem to involve linguistic intuitions that go beyond any notion of language as a mere pattern of sound waves or ink marks. In the examples immediately above, for instance, making sense of (d) seems to assume that *professor*, being a Noun, has certain things in common with *slope* or *Wug* that it does not share with *enjoy* or *up*. The whole question of linguistic nominalism then comes down to what one is to make of "Noun." On the Bloomfield-Harris model, the answer is that such categories, corresponding to nothing at the empirical level of sound waves or ink marks, are mere explanatory fictions. Or, to move to the syntactic level, consider ordering relations of the sort that turn "Susan will read Frege" into "Will Susan read Frege?" Given his methodological principles, Bloomfield has no choice but to declare that these are an unreal abstraction: "The actual sequence of constituents, and their structural order . . . are part of the language, but the descriptive order of grammatical features is a fiction and results simply from our method of describing the forms." As Katz notes, such sentiments are hauntingly similar to the instrumentalism in physical science of someone like Mach, who declared that molecules, because they cannot be seen or touched, are fictions. For if, said Mach, "to all the details of the phenomena details of the hypothesis must correspond," then "molecules are merely a valueless image" (*LOAO* 31).

This is nominalism, once again, almost in the medieval sense, the idea that everything that can be said really to exist does so at the level of concrete particulars and everything at any higher level of abstraction—one hears Quine in the background here, muttering impatiently about "mysterious meant entities"—is the empty *nomen* or name of a nonexistent entity. What Chomsky saw was that even the most routine listing of distributional regularities begins, as soon as it is generalized to unobserved instances, to point insistently to underlying principles of structure dependence, which is to say that Nouns and Verbs and the rest are not empty abstractions but entities that language itself, so to speak, treats as real. Consider, to take a standard example, the regularity evident in the inversion

(a) Susan will read Frege.
(b) Will Susan read Frege?

Suppose that we describe this inversion in Bloomfieldian terms as a regularity producing a change from declarative to interrogative mood, taking as our guide the methodological imperative that such categories as "declarative" and "interrogative" belong not to language but to our own descriptive scheme. Our generalization to uncatalogued cases will then be the principle that a first-second word inversion produces, in English, the declarative-interrogative shift. And, in fact, this seems to work well enough, permitting such examples as the change from "John will drive us" to "Will John drive us?." The problem is that a "nontheoretical" notion of regularity here soon begins producing other examples such as

(a) The literary theorist will read Frege.
(b) *Literary the theorist will read Frege?

Now this sort of example can be met well enough by patching up the notion of "regularity" to account for such problematic cases, and in fact Bloomfieldian structuralism frequently did so. But what one sees readily enough in such cases is that it is not the notion of distributional regularity *itself* that tells the linguist that patching up is needed in such cases. It is linguistic intuition—in Chomskyan terms, our competence as native speakers telling us that something has gone grammatically askew here—and the new "regularity" will silently incorporate this intuition in accounting for any new cases that do not fit the rule of simple inversion. From a Chomskyan perspective, however, what the linguist has just discovered is really a rule of deep structure that says that any Noun Phrase—"Susan," "the theorist," "the literary theorist," etc.—and modal auxiliaries ("will," "should," "must," etc.) obey an NP–AUX inversion rule that we shall look at in greater detail in a moment. Further, since the rule works *only* for modal auxiliaries, the linguist has also discovered in passing why such inversions as

(c) The literary theorist read Frege.
(d) *Read the literary theorist Frege?

are not well-formed in English. Even when glimpsed in such purely "intuitive" cases, the notion of deep structure is clearly doing important theoretical work.

Today, such examples are the stuff of introductory linguistics courses, but when Chomsky first grasped their implications in the 1950s, the effect was revolutionary. For what he had seen was not simply some new set of facts about grammar or syntax, but an underlying logic of structure and movement that permits one to glimpse linguistic rules as they are ceaselessly at work beneath the momentarily fixed surface of spoken or written utterance. This is why Chomsky's system for symbolically representing what he had seen became part of the revolution, much as *Principia* notation had operated, in logic, to give philosophers like Russell and Wittgenstein the sense that they had found a means to look "into" language for a structure hidden beneath the surface. In the case of Chomskyan grammar, the notation consists of phrase markers (P-markers) that give a formal representation of underlying structure. But this time—the point has crucial implications for Katz's related use of semantic markers—one really *is* looking into language, for the rules of deep structure thus represented are those that make even the most ordinary linguistic utterance possible. (For the notion of "looking into" language here, the example of ellipsis in chapter 2 may be helpful: recall the unseen or "invisible" second-person subject of the imperative "Dress!".)

In the present case, the P-marker for (a) above gives formal representation to a rule of structure dependence available to ordinary linguistic intuition—e.g., that *literary* "goes with" *theorist* and not with *will* or *Frege*—but, more importantly, it also permits one to "see" the most important consequence of the NP–AUX rule, namely, that *the literary theorist* must be moved, if it is to be moved at all, as a block:

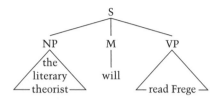

There is more. The most general implication of such examples, Chomsky saw, is that the same principle of structure dependence is at work at every level of language from phonology at the bottom to intersentential relations at the top, meaning that such traditional categories as phoneme and morpheme, Noun and Verb and Adjective, as well as such constituents as N-bar or P-bar, the discovery of which has been a direct consequence of the Chomskyan revolution, have as real an existence within the linguistic universe as, on the account given by quantum theory, do muons or pions or quarks within the physical universe. This was the shattering of the nominalist paradigm. For Zelig Harris, as one sees even more clearly in reviewing his work today, had already created most of the apparatus that would permit the construction of P-markers like that above. It remained for Chomsky to see the linguistic reality to which they so insistently pointed.

This is the sense in which the notion of deep structure, what Chomsky in 1966 ("The Current Scene in Linguistics") would describe as "the abstract underlying form which determines the meaning of the sentence," then implies a vision of language as a total system of rule-governed constituents. For it is only such a notion that, on the level of method, permits the generative grammarian to show that sentences similar in surface syntax—the examples standardly used in discussion of Chomsky's discovery of deep structure are "John is easy to please" and "John is eager to please"—mean different things because their syntax is radically dissimilar at the level of deep structure. At a more general level, the same conception permitted Chomsky to redefine grammar as a specification of the rules that then generate all and only the well-formed sentences in a language.

The notion of deep structure as a level demanded by an adequate theory of linguistic phenomena has the strange effect of turning on their head all Wittgenstein's injunctions against trying to see "beneath the surface," searching for "something that lies within, which we see when we looking *into* the thing, and which an analysis brings out." For such analysis will be, on Chomsky's account of language, not a caveat but a methodological imperative, what one *must* do if one wants genuinely to understand language on its own terms. The same will be true of Quine's objections, in "Two Dogmas" and the famous "gavagai" example in *Word and Object*, that meanings are in their invisibility—by which he would have meant lack of conditions for objective individuation on behavioral grounds—something akin to Homer's gods. Katz's answer is that Quine has the wrong sort of invisibility here. The invisibility of constituent elements in Chomsky's theory of syntax or Katz's own theory of sense structure is, in fact, much more like the invisibility of Neptune when early astronomers were compelled to posit its existence from observed perturbations in the orbit of Uranus. The analogy is deeply Chomskyan in spirit.

Several points emerge from Chomsky's original formulation of the transformational or generative program that are crucial to the way Katz will conceive of the New Intensionalism in semantic theory. The most important concerns the nature of Chomsky's theory as what both he and Katz call a "top down" approach to explaining linguistic phenomena. In its original signification, which was meant to contrast Chomsky's method with the "bottom up" approach of Bloomfield and others—that purely inductive approach that, as we have seen, thinks it is merely collecting and cataloguing distributional regularities in a corpus of utterance—the "top down" notion is easy enough to grasp. But it has implications that very soon point beyond that original signification. I have already used a chess analogy. This has a venerable status in linguistics—Saussure speaks in the *Cours générale* of the "grammar" of chess—but here the point lies solely in the way a self-contained system of rules is able to generate a near-infinity of actual games. Part of what is implied by "top down" thus has to do with the way a simple set of constraints may be shown to govern a huge and otherwise bewildering range of actual chess moves or actual utterances.

A second point raised by deep structure involves a dispute between Chomsky and Katz on which I shall do no more than touch: the issue of whether linguistics is the study of language acquisition (Chomsky) or the study of language-as-system (Katz). Still, one of Chomsky's original arguments for the existence of UG or universal grammar—a kind of abstract "language behind languages"—is a great aid to understanding Katz's own theory. Chomsky put this argument in terms of language acquisition. For the astounding fact is that language really is in some

67

sense universal: a child raised in France will grow up speaking French, but the same child removed at an early age to Japan will grow up speaking Japanese. Chomsky's inference is that the child is born with an LAD or Language Acquisition Device programmed to master any language fed into it. Katz's will be that the various natural languages are simply contingent embodiments of Language as a universal system. These are very different conclusions, but in both cases the idea of universality derives ultimately from the notion of deep structure.

Finally, the element of the Chomskyan revolution that carries over most directly into Katz's New Intensionalism is the awareness, admitted by Chomsky even in the early days when he most strongly insisted on a purely formalist view of generative grammar—i.e., that grammaticality as generated by syntactic rules was to be thought of in wholly formal terms, on analogy with theorems in logic or proof in mathematics—that a theory of language involving deep structure could never, except by arbitrary fiat, sever syntax from semantics. Outside linguistics, this is known to most people as the famous puzzle of how syntactically well-formed sentences are to be taken when they are semantically anomalous—*colorless green ideas sleep furiously*—but this is really the problem in its least interesting aspect.

Any introductory textbook in modern linguistics contains hundreds of examples in which semantic considerations are silently taken into account when syntax is analyzed. Thus, for instance—the example is adapted from from Radford, as is that concerning disambiguation below—it is normal when talking about categories and structure dependence to note that the "same word" may appear in different syntactic categories, as with *need* here:

(a) Does he *need* to see a doctor? [Verb]
(b) *Need* he be there? [Modal]
(c) I feel a *need* to explore my roots [Noun]

Saussure's notion of a grammar of chess comes once again to mind, for what Saussure said is that chess pieces like knights or pawns are assigned their "value" by the rules. The analogy suggests something of the way in which the semantic value of *need* is here being variously assigned by syntactic rules.

Such examples suggest that syntax, which in *colorless green ideas sleep furiously* can be imagined to be somehow operating independent of semantic content, more often determines meaning at the most ele-

mentary level. (When one gives students an OED exercise on a Shakespeare sonnet or a Marvell lyric, the mistake they will most commonly
make is to look up, for instance, the noun form of a word that occurs
as an adjective or verb in the poetic line: semantic incomprehension
owing to an error of syntactic analysis.) The same inseparability of syntactic and semantic considerations is evident in cases of what is conventionally treated as purely structural ambiguity, as in the sentence:

(1) The President could not ratify the treaty.

Ordinary linguistic intuition will allow any native speaker to "hear"
the ambiguity here, and a moment's reflection will then suggest that
the ambiguity somehow depends on how *not* is understood as func-
tioning syntactically. But linguistic intuition will not by itself bring to
light the grammatical rules underlying what is called the scope ambiguity here. A rough and ready way of doing so is to use a pseudo-cleft
construction as a test, formulating (1) as

(1a) What the President *could not* do is ratify the treaty.
(1b) What the President could do is *not ratify* the treaty.

This works well enough as a testing procedure, but we are still at some
distance from isolating anything that could be called a grammatical
rule. Here we have precisely the sort of case in which the P-markers of
Chomsky's system assume a great importance in establishing the notion of deep structure. For what the P-markers do is allow us to see the
underlying structure that produces the ambiguity:

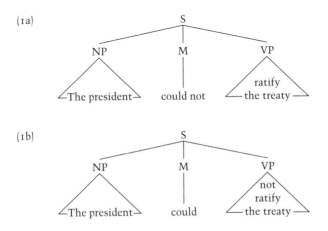

Now, once again, we are in a situation where syntax is not easily separated from semantics. To represent the alternatives in this way is to treat the ambiguity in purely syntactic terms as a scope ambiguity— i.e., as turning on the scope of *not* as a negative particle—and yet our ordinary tendency to say that the two sentences *mean* different things is, surely, to say something just as important. This is a point that Katz will simply assume in treating his own theory of decompositional sense structure not merely as something authorized by or modeled on Chomskyan grammar, but as an extension of it. For what Chomsky saw when he looked through the surface of a corpus of observed utterances to an underlying set of linguistic rules was not a realm of purely syntactic possibility, but one in which sound and structure and meaning, phonology and syntax and semantics, are always in simultaneous operation.

It is useful to recall, at this point, that the roots of Katz's New Intensionalism lie in his original attempts, working mainly with Jerry Fodor, to work out in rigorous or systematic terms a semantics for Chomskyan generative grammar. Many elements of that original project survive in Katz's present theory, but one of obvious interest here is the notion of a "universal" semantic field—the idea has obvious affinities with Chomsky's idea of universal grammar as discussed above—and the way this was associated with the semantic notation of Katz and Fodor, in which, for instance, a concept like HUMAN was so represented to show that the distinction between human and non-human constitutes a major semantic category in every natural language. Or, to take another well-known example from the days of Katz-Fodor marker notation, one could ask whether a verb like *kill* was a semantic primitive or must be understood in decompositional terms as combining the more primitive senses of *cause* and *die*:

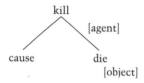

The significance of the early Katz-Fodor work on sense representation is that it seemed so obviously to restore to intelligibility what we have heard Quine contemptuously dismiss as "language-independent meanings." The notion that such meanings exist is something that ordinary intuition finds plausible enough. When I am in France speaking French or Germany speaking German I normally think of myself as trying to say "the same thing" that at home I would say in English under similar circumstances. The same intuition underlies our assurance to beginning language students that *il pleut* and *es regnet* and *it's raining* mean the same thing. But this is an intuition that has not held up very well in the face of Quinean skepticism or Wittgenstein's intricate and highly original ways of getting one to see meaning as always dissolving into some context of use.

In linguistic theory, one has to go back to the Port Royal grammar—to which Katz gracefully acknowledges a debt—to discover anything like the idea of a universal "language of thought" lying behind natural languages. This is why, in undertaking to resurrect the idea in modern semantics, Katz will place an enormous emphasis on the idea that meaning is *compositional*: just as words are built up out of phonemes or sentences out of words, complex meanings are built up out of simpler meanings. For this is an essential idea in every version of modern linguistic theory, and here its effect is precisely to demonstrate that meaning is always in a certain sense language-independent. Katz's favorite example is *starve*, taken in its sense of dying from hunger or a lack of food. As it happens, there is a semantic asymmetry here: English has no parallel word—that is, on the analogy of *hungry* ↔ *thirsty*—meaning to die from thirst or lack of water. And there may well be natural languages in which this word exists. But this is a meaning that English permits me to express effortlessly enough should I need to simply by combining the senses of already-existing words. Indeed, in the phrase "to die from thirst or lack of water" I have just done so.

The notion of compositionality is, as we shall see, enormously important to the way Katz handles various features of semantic structure, but just as important from another point of view is the domain of language-independent or language-neutral meanings towards which *starve* and similar examples point. For along with the notion of compositionality, it is the notion of maximally generalized semantic categories—again, HUMAN as represented in Katz-Fodor marker notation—that is carried forward in the intensionalist program Katz has been more recently developing. The concept of the "most general" semantic category survives, as we shall see, in the way Katz's theory represents superordination and subordination relations within decompositional sense structure.

We will look at an example of the way Katz's semantic markers display such relations in a moment, but I want to emphasize before we do so the sense in which Katz's symbolic representations will always be exploiting an intuitive awareness of superordination and decompositional structure without which we could scarcely negotiate the world. Katz's emphasis will always be purely linguistic. Any adequate formal representation of *dwelling/cottage,* for instance, would have to show that the higher-level semantic category *dwelling* is superordinate to *cottage, mansion, barracks,* etc. Yet in fact, this is the way thought seems to work as well. One might say, if it were not for that psychologism to which Katz is rightly opposed, that one never simply grasps an isolated concept as such, but always and simultaneously a descending and ascending order of relations: Object $\longrightarrow$ Physical $\longrightarrow$ Artifact $\longrightarrow$ Furniture $\longrightarrow$ Table $\longrightarrow$ coffee table $\longrightarrow$ mahogany coffee table $\longrightarrow$ mahogany-coffee-table-with-Uncle-Leonard's-cigarette-burn (etc.).

Such examples get at part of what Katz has in mind by decompositional sense structure, but they leave out the single most important fact about that structure, which is that it is held together by entailment relations. In fact, such relations will just be what Katz *means* by semantic entailment. A thing could not be a table without being furniture, and could not be furniture without being a physical object. To understand *table* is to understand these entailments. Such relations hold not just from the top to the bottom of the structure, but, as we shall shortly see, across categories within the structure as well. In this sense, semantic entailment may be imagined as the simultaneous set of relations sustaining the structure *as* a structure.

In Katz's symbolic representation of sense structure, two features are taken over more or less intact from Chomskyan grammar. The first is that syntactic function is always prior to semantic value: in formal terms, this will give us the role of Chomskyan grammatical functions in Katz's semantic markers. I will explain these below. In informal terms, however, this is the feature of Katz's theory that gives us an account of what our students are doing when, at work in the library on a Shakespeare or Donne poem, they see that they must decide whether the word in the poetic line is a noun or a verb before choosing the relevant OED definition. The second feature, which is that of c-command, is silently incorporated into Katz's marker system and needs no separate discussion here. A convenient example from Chomskyan grammar is the way a tree diagram represents as top-to-bottom directionality the way, say, a singular subject has the power to "choose" the singular form of a verb.

A major problem with trying to give readers a sense of how Katz's semantic markers work is that his most elaborately worked-out examples in recent years have been produced in connection with philosophical problems like Descartes' *cogito* or Davidson's analysis of action sentences. This is because Katz's main interest has been in demonstrating various ways in which philosophy has wandered into blind alleys for lack of any satisfactory account of analytic entailment. Yet the examples constructed in Katz's earlier work and summarized in purely linguistic terms in books like *Semantic Theory* demand, out of a fairness to him, a more detailed acquaintance with his larger system than can be aimed for here. Let me take, then, one of the more "detachable" of his recent philosophical examples, the semantic representation for the verb *chase* as he discusses it in "Common Sense in Semantics":

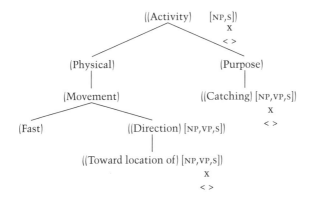

As I have said, the aim is to try to give the reader a feel for how semantic representations like this one operate without going in any great detail into Katz's larger system. What I want to do is isolate one simple feature of the notation and then step back and try to "see" the entire representation. The feature is the syntactic symbol in square brackets beside various of the concept categories: [NP,S] as it occurs beside (Activity), for instance, or [NP,VP,S] beside (Catching) or (Direction). These are grammatical functions taken over directly from

Chomsky: *functions* because phrasal constituents can play various roles which therefore must be specified. In *The policeman chased the demonstrators,* the Noun Phrase or NP *the policeman* functions as a subject, hence [NP,S] in Chomsky's notation. In *The demonstrators chased the policeman,* on the other hand, *the policeman* functions as a direct object ([NP,VP,S]). So [NP,S] beside (Activity) simply specifies that any noun or noun phrase inserted at this point must function as the subject of the verb.

A very long way around, one might be forgiven for thinking, to arrive at something one might have found in an eighth-grade grammar book: verbs have subjects. And this will also be true when the two noun phrases in *The policeman chased the demonstrators* are substituted in appropriate places in the semantic representation. (Try it nonetheless: mentally substitute *the policeman* where you see [NP,S] and *the demonstrators* in each place you see [NP,VP,S]). And it will be true, finally, when one realizes that everything now left over is a semantic analysis of the verb *chase*: who could not have told that the meaning of *chase* has to do with the physical pursuit of one person or thing by another with the ultimate aim of catching him or her or it? Some formal notations, such as predicate logic or even transformational grammar, can be daunting to the uninitiated because they look mysterious or hermetic. Katz's, on the contrary, can appear overly complicated just because it seems to go to such lengths to symbolize the obvious.

Nothing could be farther from the truth, but seeing why demands seeing in a certain way. Look again at the semantic representation above. The [NP,S] and [NP,VP,S] brackets are there first of all, as I've said, to show the priority of syntax over semantics. (This is why, once again, a student working on a poem will need to determine whether *need* is a noun or a verb before understanding its semantic value in the poetic line.) But now, having made the mental substitutions of *the policeman* and *the demonstrators* that I asked you to make, look again, this time for the verb of the sentence. What you will see, if you are looking in the way Katz's theory wants you to look, is that *there is no verb in the sentence.* Where the verb should be, holding [NP,S]———[NP,VP,S]—alternatively, *the policeman* [ ] *the demonstrators*—together in a determinate way, is what might be called a network of sense relations governed by ordering principles such as superordination, subordination, and entailment.

It would be entirely in the spirit of Katz's program to say that what the representation has therefore done is to dissolve the verb *chase* into the decompositional sense structure that is its underlying semantic form. Or one might say, on analogy with those "exploded" diagrams that aim to make motors or machines comprehensible to the weekend mechanic, that it is an exploded view of the same structure. The analogy does not matter so long as one has seen that the whole point of the semantic representation is to make *chase* disappear as a syntactic simple so that the complex reality of its sense structure may suddenly leap into view. When one has seen this, one will see simultaneously why Katz's markers so often give the feeling of representing what we already knew. That is his point: we have always known this, and yet we have not been struck with the momentousness of what we knew.

That momentousness lies for Katz in the solution of various philosophical problems that cannot, on his view, be solved without the notion of semantic entailment. For our purposes here, it will be enough to take notice of certain features of the semantic representation. First, then, note that the place of (Activity) at the topmost node for *chase* gives us the level of generality or abstraction brought forward, in a certain sense, from Katz-Fodor marker notation. In general terms, an awareness that one climbs a "ladder of generality" in thinking one's way upward through orders of superordination—table → furniture → physical → object, etc.—has, no doubt, had implications for philosophy from Plato onwards. Katz's point will always be that, no matter what its philosophical implications, it is built right into the structure of language.

Two other features of the marker, the x and the empty brackets ⟨⟩ attached to certain concept categories, may be noted in passing. In brief, x plus the syntactic categorization yields a recursive specification permitting complex semantic wholes to be built up from simpler ones. This is a standard feature of linguistic theories. (An example of recursive specification at the syntactic level: *Ed said that Cora kissed him; Bruce swore that Ed said that Cora kissed him; Marc reported that Bruce swore that Ed said,* etc.) The empty brackets are selectors that "filter" semantic substitutions to block meaningless constructions: the *colorless green ideas sleep furiously* problem as Katz solves it, en passant, with category specification. An example is the way (Physical) in the marker above selects entities like policemen, demonstrators, dogs, cats, etc., while screening out non-physical objects like prime numbers or nouns. What the brackets here exclude is such possibilities as *The prime number chased the noun all the way home.*

For any account of what actually goes one when students are given a Donne poem and an OED assignment, a more important feature of the marker is the way the category concepts in the superordination structure operate at a lateral level of implication. Thus, for instance, (Physical) as we have seen works top-to-bottom to select [NP,S] and [NP,VP,S] such that something physical will always be chasing something physical. But the same specification works on its own category level to exclude everything in the vast superordinate category (Activity) that is not also physical. This excludes, for instance, activities like daydreaming, planning a picnic, or solving a chess problem. In the same way, (Movement) selects for physical activities that involve a change of location or position (jogging, walking, chasing demonstrators) as opposed to those that do not (playing the piano, doing pushups). Or, to borrow an example directly from Katz, (Fast) both excludes activities in the next-higher category for which no speed is specified (walking), and those specified as being slow (creeping).

To "see" a semantic representation in Katzian terms is to see a constellation of senses held together as though in a gravitational field. For Katzian entailment relations do in fact operate as a sort of linguistic version of gravitational action-at-a-distance. The "bond" that creates such clusters as *table* → *furniture* → *object*, or the entailment that produces a pair like *chase* → *follow*, are features of what are now in linguistics called—though often in areas very far away from Katzian semantics, it should be said—principles of government and binding. For Katz himself, as I have said, the implications of such semantic relations have in recent years seemed most importantly to be philosophical. This is, once again, Quine's "All bachelors are unmarried" as a problem of analytic entailment for which standard logic is unable to give an account.

To see how the problem works in terms of the present example, note simply that *The policeman chased the demonstrators* seems, to any competent speaker of English, in some obviously necessary sense to entail *The policeman followed the demonstrators.* But why? Where is the intuition that an entailment must somehow be involved here—and, moreover, that it must be a necessary entailment, the strongest permitted in standard logic—coming from?

To see where it is coming from is by Katz's lights suddenly to have been given a key to a whole set of major problems that twentieth-century philosophers, trapped within the much narrower notion of entailment permitted them by traditional and modern logic, have been able to see only as a source of puzzlement or frustration.

Katz's recent work on analyticity, which belongs to philosophy rather than linguistics, would soon carry us away from the concerns of the present book. I want to end this chapter, however, by looking at one failed attempt—Carnap's—to deal with such entailments in the standard manner, because it has implications for an understanding of Katz's linguistic realism as I shall discuss it in the epilogue. Carnap was an original and resourceful logician but, if we reserve the term for anyone whose logical program has no place for analytic entailment, he was also a "classical" logician in the sense Katz means to emphasize. This is why Carnap, troubled by the innumerable entailments in ordinary language that seem to depend on semantic relations among items in the extra-logical vocabulary, would try to solve the problem by expanding the predicate calculus to account for them. The result was the famous meaning postulates of later Carnapian theory. Once again, the problem is to show why *The policeman chased the demonstrators* seems "necessarily" to entail *The policeman followed the demonstrators*. Here is Carnap's attempt to give formal represenation to the entailment:

$$(x)\,(y)\,(Cx,y \supset Fx,y)$$

The horseshoe is the standard *"if . . . then"* of material implication, and C and F are predicate-like designations regimenting *chase* and *follow*. The reason that the policeman who chased the demonstrators followed the demonstrators, in short, is that Carnap has set up a situation in which any individual x who chases y will also necessarily follow y. Against this project Quine brought two devastating criticisms. One is that because Carnap's postulates employ particular lexical items from a language, they are in principle unable to explain the general, language-independent notion of analyticity. The other is that Carnap's postulates merely *stipulate* which sentences of a language are to be counted as having the property of analyticity, while failing to explain what that property is. The list of sentences stipulated by Carnap as "analytic-for-L_o," Quine famously said, would better be labelled as "K" so as not to seem to throw light on the interesting word "analytic."

For Katz, the crucial point is that Carnap is unable to define analyticity because, trying to operate within the confines of a logical system able only to represent entailment relations among propositions, he has no way of seeing that *chase* has a decompositional structure that already contains the sense of *follow*. The problem of *The policeman chased the demonstrators* as this entails *The policeman followed the demonstrators* is solved, within Katz's system of semantic representation, simply by seeing that, as we immediately observe if we look closely at the earlier semantic representation, *follow* is already contained by *chase* as a same-rooted subtree of the original marker:

((Activity) [NP,S])
    | X
(Physical)$^{<\ >}$
    |
(Movement)
    |
(Direction)
    |
((Toward location of)
    [NP,S]
    X
    < >

In such works as *The Metaphysics of Meaning*, Katz will see the main point of such examples as having to do with various philosophical problems to which he sees a strong theoretical account of semantic entailment as the obvious solution. For those in literary studies, however, the greater significance will seem to lie in the the otherwise invisible system of semantic relations made visible by the marker. These relations permit Katz to develop a notion of type meaning that, as we saw in chapter two, imposes constraints on token meaning in any situation in which utterance takes place. For speech act theory like that of Austin or Searle or Grice, this will be the situation in which ordinary people talk to each other. For literary theory, as we shall see, it will be the situation in which the Duke in Browning's *My Last Duchess* addresses the emissary of a neighboring nobleman, or in which the speaker of Donne's *Elegy XIX* urges his lover to hurry with her undressing.

I want to return to the problem of determinate meaning by looking at several of Stanley Fish's arguments in *Is There a Text in This Class?*, which I do partly by way of compliment to that book. For while I do not think his account of meaning can survive Katz's analysis of the type-token relation, Fish deserves credit for having been over the last twenty years virtually the only important literary theorist to remain in touch with linguistics and philosophy of language. Nor am I thinking simply about his awareness of Chomskyan grammar or Austin-Searle speech act theory. During a period when what has counted as "theory" in English departments has so often been an intellectual embarrassment, Fish has consistently brought to literary theory something of the energy and clarity associated with Anglo-American analytic philosophy.

Fish has two standard moves against the notion of meaning as something prior to or independent of interpretation. The first is the simple equation of linguistic meaning with social convention, and as such does not concern us here. (The reason is that one could agree that a social convention like handshaking was meaningless "in itself" and still have good grounds for thinking that linguistic meaning existed on entirely different terms.) The other, to which we may now turn with Katz's treatment of the type-token relation in mind, consists of imagining new pragmatic situations in which an apparently unambiguous meaning suddenly becomes ambiguous. So, for instance, Fish borrows from a linguistic textbook an example of an "inherently" ambiguous sentence—

(a) The suit is too light to wear.

—which the authors then suppose themselves to be disambiguating by expanding the sentence as follows:

(b) The suit is too light to wear on such a cold day.

One sees readily enough what is going on here. The ambiguity is supposed to turn on *light*, as having the sense either of "light in color" or "light in weight"—a perfect demonstration, it should be noted, of why Katz sees senses as entities necessary to account for ambiguity—and talk about cold weather is then supposed to block one of these by specifying weight or warmth of fabric. But then Fish imagines himself in dialogue with his wife, more fashion-conscious than he, who thinks that light-colored suits ought to be worn only in the warm months. So *light* in (b) may now again refer to color. Similarly, Fish borrows from M. F. Garrett another sentence containing *light* that has been supposed to be unambiguous—"This stuff is light enough to carry"—and gives Garrett's scenario for shifting the sense from weight to color:

> Scene: Highway patrolman lecturing to 3rd grade class.
> Patrolman: "When you are walking on a highway at night, it is important to wear light colored clothing or carry a light colored flag so that you will be visible to oncoming cars. For instance (holds up flag), this stuff is light enough to carry." (qtd. in *TITC* 282)

The trick, as will be evident, is to identify meaning with pragmatic meaning and then to produce as many "meanings" as one can invent speech act situations. Fish used this approach with great ingenuity over a period of years, abandoning it, one suspects, only when he had begun to sense that diminishing returns had set in. A moment's consideration will show why returns were bound to diminish. To *begin* a discussion with the assumption that linguistic meaning is identical to speech-act meaning is to beg the whole question of whether language may be said to have meanings or senses apart from pragmatic contexts. This is a limitation that comes into especially sharp focus in light of Katz's interpretation of the type-token relation, including his account of meaning at the token level as involving "pragmatic scatter."

We looked at an example in chapter two when discussing Frege's idea that questions contain a proposition *and* an interrogative or erotetic element. Wittgenstein's countermove, it will be recalled, was to give an example of meaning-as-use. Since we may use "Isn't the weather glorious today?" to *say* that the weather is glorious today, Frege's notion of an unseen or "hidden" erotetic element must be an illusion. And Katz's rejoinder was that that Frege had it right: "Isn't the weather glorious today?" really does have an interrogative or erotetic element written right into its syntax at the *type* level. What Wittgenstein had shown was simply that type and token meaning do not always coincide, as when, having seen that I know perfectly well that the weather is glorious, and that there is no place for a genuine question here, you correctly take me to be uttering a polite conventionality.

The notion of pragmatic scatter as a non-coincidence of type and token meaning serves to explain why Katz sees a well-developed pragmatic theory to be an indispensable complement to intensional semantics. For while Chomskyan syntactic rules or Katz's own theory of decompositional sense structure explain meaning at the type level, they do not explain the way type meaning may then be twisted, inverted, altered, or deflected at the token level. In principle, Katz makes clear, any sophisticated pragmatic theory might be brought in to demonstrate what his theory will mean by pragmatic scatter. His own interest as an intensionalist is in the way the process is governed in a "top down" way by type meaning. Having said as much, he then takes his examples in *The Metaphysics of Meaning* from a single influential pragmatic theory, Grice's theory of conversational implicature.

The particular magic of Gricean conversational implicature is that it seems to direct one's gaze past the utterance to a body of rules invisibly operating in the background. Suppose, for instance, that I tell you that "Either George or Harry said that X." On Grice's account, I "conversationally implicate" that I do not know which of the two it was. But this is not something that logic permits you, strictly speaking, to infer from my utterance. In purely logical terms, if I happen to *know* that it was George who said X, I may quite correctly assert that the person who did so was either George or Harry. It was, after all, one of the two. Nor is the inference one we could derive from even the most exhaustive syntactic or semantic description of the utterance. On Grice's account, such "invisible" rules of implicature are always there in the background, making merely linguistic meaning come alive in the pragmatic contexts of actual utterance.

Katz's point even about pragmatic theories as subtle as Grice's will be that they are unable to give an account of the way in which Language— I use the capital L to signal that we are now in the world of Peirce's ideal types—is controlling the whole process from the top down. For pragmatic theories want ultimately to imply, as Fish's examples demonstrate, that one can make an utterance mean quite literally anything one wants by altering the contingencies of the speech act situation. Thus a pure pragmatism becomes something like Humpty Dumpty's position in the famous conversation *Through the Looking Glass*:

> "I don't know what you mean by 'glory,'" Alice said.
>
> Humpty Dumpty smiled contemptuously. "Of course you don't—till I tell you. I meant 'there's a nice knock-down argument for you!'"
>
> "But 'glory' doesn't mean 'a nice knock-down argument,'" Alice objected.
>
> "When *I* use a word," Humpty Dumpty said, in rather a scornful tone, "it means just what I choose it to mean—neither more nor less."
>
> "The question is," said Alice, "whether you *can* make words mean so many different things."
>
> "The question is," said Humpty Dumpty, "which is to be master—that's all." (163)

Katz's point will be that, no matter how bizarre the results one can obtain by imagining variations in the pragmatic situation (Fish's speciality), utterance within the speech-act context must still consist of linguistic *tokens* which sustain a determinate relation to a *type* existing outside or beyond that context. It is the determinacy of the relation that sets limits to pragmatic scatter. If, to adapt one of Katz's own examples, I remark to you that "George is a fine friend," I have just uttered a sentiment that on the type-level implies that George possesses certain admirable qualities such as loyalty, selflessness, and the like. And in any situation in which it is used literally—you know that George has just saved me from bankruptcy by lending me a large amount of money interest-free—this will be its token or pragmatic meaning as well. Such examples demonstrate Katz's point that literalness just is a coincidence of type and token meaning. But in a situation in which the pragmatic context is altered—e.g., you know that George has just burned down my house and run off with my wife—the relation between type and token will alter correspondingly, with the token now meaning something like "George is a rotten friend."

In this situation we should normally be disposed to speak not simply of my meaning but of my bitterness or irony. As they get at the complexities of the pragmatic situation such terms are wholly appropriate. But what Katz wants us to see is that the semantic reversal through which "George is a fine friend" comes to mean "George is a rotten friend" is *still* being controlled by the type-token relation. The ironic implication "rotten" is created as a pragmatic possibility solely through an inversion of the type meaning of "fine." To see that this is so, it is necessary only to compare "George is a fine friend" with, for instance, "George is an old friend," which in the case of such betrayal would express simple pain or disbelief. Such examples show why, for the New Intensionalism, theories like those of Austin or Searle or Grice reveal their full explanatory power precisely when they are enlisted in the project of mapping pragmatic scatter.

The examples Katz uses to illustrate pragmatic scatter in *The Metaphysics of Meaning* are usually single utterances of the "George is a fine friend" variety, and these are, in fact, the sort of examples favored by Fish in *Is There a Text in this Class?* and elsewhere. This raises the issue of why Fish chooses to concentrate on single utterances. For Katz, such a choice is obvious: he wants to show how type meaning operates in a "top down" way to impose constraints on token utterance. But Fish, we can imagine someone objecting—the issue has been raised several times in commentary on his work—is supposed to be a literary theorist. Why, instead of isolated sentences taken from linguistics textbooks, doesn't he use lines from, to take our example in chapter 1, a poem like Donne's *Valediction: Forbidding Mourning*?

The reason, it seems to me, is that a poem like the *Valediction* is *already* a pragmatic or speech act situation in which interpretation must operate by simultaneously determining sense structure at the type level and mapping pragmatic scatter within the dramatic situation. In chapter 1 I included a student handout that goes to some length to demonstrate that a single phrase in the third stanza—*moving of th'earth*—may be shown to mean one thing rather than another, X rather than Y. But now it is crucial to note that that analysis was simply taking for granted something equally important, which is that the speaker of the poem is a man addressing a woman who wishes he were not about to leave her to go on a journey:

> *Dull sublunary lovers' love,*
> *(Whose soul is sense) cannot admit*
> *Absence, because it doth remove*
> *Those things which elemented it.*

> But we, by a love so much refined
> That ourselves know not what it is,
> Inter-assured of the mind,
> Care less, eyes, lips, and hands to miss.

For students just beginning with poetry, syntax and meaning at the type level present the greatest obstacles to comprehension. This is why one goes to great lengths to make sure, for instance, that everyone in the class understands that the first occurrence of *it* takes as its antecedent *absence*, and the second the *love* of *dull sublunary lovers' love*, and the third *love* in *a love so much refined*. This is pure syntactic analysis, very often at the traditional and sometimes—as in the case of ellipsis and related phenomena—at the Chomskyan level. Then one goes to similarly great lengths not only to see that students have found their way to the relevant meaning of *sublunary* in the *OED*, but also that they have then begun to imagine to themselves the whole Renaissance myth of perfection and imperfection implied by it: the "pure regions above the moon," and the related notion of terrestrial or sublunary life as subject to change, growth, death, and decay.

During the period of close reading inaugurated by Cleanth Brooks's *The Well Wrought Urn*, analysis of the pragmatic or speech-act situation "inside" the poem always played a central role in literary interpretation. Yet apart from one very brief discussion in Wimsatt and Beardsley's *The Verbal Icon*, pragmatic analysis as such never commanded much theoretical attention. The reason, I suggested in the preface, had to do with the tacit dimension (to borrow Polanyi's term again) of New Critical interpretation. Close reading takes the pragmatic situation silently into account when working out meaning at the type level. One sees this when teaching Donne's *Valediction*. No student who has understood the syntactic relations involved in the three occurrences of *it*, and that *sublunary* involves not simply the sense "earthly, imperfect" but a whole different way of imagining the cosmos, will then fail to have understood that the speaker is a man of a certain age and social class speaking to a woman upset by his going away, or that this man and woman are either young married people or lovers newly on terms of physical intimacy.

The experience of teaching a poem like the *Valediction* to students illustrates another important point. This is that any error concerning syntax or semantics at the type level almost invariably leads—in just

the way that Katz's account of pragmatic scatter might be taken to pre-
dict—to a mistaken analysis of the pragmatic situation "inside" the
poem. A student who has not seen that *as* in the first line of Donne's
Valediction announces a simile or extended comparison, for instance,
will very often take the entire poem to be the utterance of an old man
contemplating his own death. A tiny error in syntactic analysis is thus
able to produce gross misreading at the token or utterance level. Nonetheless, error at the token or pragmatic level is its own category. A
reader who takes the speaker of the *Valediction* to be an eighty-year-
old man addressing his four-year-old niece has misread the poem in a
different way than someone who misunderstands an antecedent of *it*
or the relevant sense of *sublunary*.

During the period of New Critical ascendancy, the only attempt to
give an account of determinate meaning in the way now suggested
by Katz's intensional semantics was Monroe Beardsley's in *The Possibility of Criticism*. For Beardsley, familiar as a philosopher with
speech act theory as it had then begun to emerge, tried to give a provi-
sional account of literary works as complex illocutionary acts, and to
show that type meaning in Katz's sense always imposes constraints
on token or pragmatic meaning in literary contexts. Yet Beardsley had
no real vocabulary for talking either about sense structure or pragmatic
scatter on the Katz type-token model. His way of describing determinate meaning, almost poignant in retrospect, was, for instance, to say
that "macromeanings" in interpretation must emerge in demonstrable
terms from "micromeanings." Moreover, his book was written too late
in the day to have any real impact.

As I have already tried to suggest, however, it may have been a very
good thing that pragmatic theory in linguistics and philosophy did
not develop rapidly enough to provide an account of what literary critics were doing when analyzing a poem like Donne's *Valediction* as a
complex speech act. For the mode of analysis exemplified in a work
like Brooks's *The Well Wrought Urn* was already operating at a level of
far greater sophistication than would subsequently develop in speech
act theory. This is something one clearly sees when recalling, for instance, the delight with which philosophers were wont to discuss certain examples of Gricean conversational implicature when they first
appeared. Here is one. You and I are philosophy professors walking
across the quad, and I recall that a student named Smithers, who is

this semester taking my medieval philosophy course, was in your epistemology class last term. So I ask you about him, and you reply "Mr. Smithers is invariably punctual and has excellent handwriting."

There is wit in this, and real analytic or philosophical content as well. For if I see that you have just "conversationally implicated" that Smithers is substandard as a student of philosophy, it will be because (1) there are rules according to which I may interpret what you have said as a meaningful utterance rather than a non sequitur, and (2) I have understood that you mean me to apply these rules to your remark about Smithers. But this sort of thing is primitive compared to what a competent reader is called upon to do when reading a Henry James short story or Congreve's *The Way of the World* or a passage like this one from Browning's *My Last Duchess*:

> She thanked men—good! but thanked
> Somehow—I know not how—as if she ranked
> My gift of a nine-hundred-years-old name
> With anybody's gift. Who'd stoop to blame
> This sort of trifling? Even had you skill
> In speech—which I have not—to make your will
> Quite clear to such an one, and say, "Just this
> "Or that in you disgusts me; here you miss,
> "Or there exceed the mark"—and if she let
> Herself be lessoned so, nor plainly set
> Her wits to yours, forsooth, and made excuse,
> —E'en then would be some stooping; and I choose
> Never to stoop.

One enters at such a moment a world teeming with pragmatic implication. The challenge of teaching *My Last Duchess* to students is, along with analysis of syntax and the OED definitions, seeing how much of it they can be brought to grasp on their own. Most will have seen, for instance, that the speaker is a Duke of the Italian Renaissance, a man of obsessive, almost delusional pride in his name and lineage. Most will also have seen that the conversation we are overhearing takes place in an upper storey of the Duke's villa, and that downstairs is gathered a party of visitors composed of a neighboring nobleman, a Count, and those traveling with him, including his daughter. Some—but only some—will have seen that the conversation is between the Duke and an emissary of this Count—a steward or attorney or private secretary—and that the subject of the conversation is the marriage now being arranged between the Duke and the Count's daughter, who, if things work out, will be his "next" duchess.

Yet most students will not have seen—will only see as the class is ending—that the Duke's whole speech to the emissary has been an elaborately indirect warning about the behavior he will expect from his next wife. For the poem begins as what sounds like an innocent exercise in art appreciation, as the Duke draws back the curtain from Frà Pandolf's portrait of his last duchess, a lovely and innocent young woman whose only crime was that she did not pay exclusive enough reverence to him and his ancient lineage. Only toward the end of the speech does one come to see that one is dealing with a dark and twisted mind, that the Duke is telling the emissary, all but openly, that he had his young wife done away with for failing to pay him the exclusive attention to which he supposes himself entitled:

> *Oh sir, she smiled, no doubt,*
> *Whene'er I passed her; but who passed without*
> *Much the same smile? This grew; I gave commands;*
> *Then all smiles stopped together.*

And this, the Duke not being a man who wants more bother of the same sort, is the message the emissary is supposed to carry back to the Count his master.

Now everything that is going on in *My Last Duchess* seems to me to be explicable in terms of pragmatic scatter, which is why, as I shall attempt to show in a moment, I think Katz's interpretation of the type-token relation holds the solution to the problem of determinate meaning in literary theory. Yet I want in the strongest terms to make clear that I do not think this is a case where "theory" is needed. The beginning of sound philosophical analysis, Wittgenstein said at a time when philosophers were much preoccupied with logical notation, was to see that everything is all right with ordinary language just as it is. That is my point about close reading in literary interpretation: the interpretive method used by Brooks in *The Well Wrought Urn*, or Dorothy Van Ghent in *The English Novel*, was a powerful means of understanding literary works as self-contained worlds with their own laws and their own logic. Literary studies as a discipline should ask for nothing more.

The best way of teaching students to read *A Valediction: Forbidding*

Mourning or *My Last Duchess* will continue to be, in short, to send them to the OED, and to analyze poetic syntax until they are certain that they understand the grammatical function of every word. The entire value of Katz's New Intensionalism is simply that it demonstrates the sense in which the linguistic system carries within itself— to recall the terms I used in chapter I—the means to determine that a word or a phrase means one thing rather than another, X rather than Y. Then, given Katz's interpretation of the type-token relation and the notion of pragmatic scatter, one is also given a means of understanding the ways in which errors at the level of primary meaning inevitably produce errors in second-order interpretation. This is "theory," in short, as it leaves everything already occurring in sound literary interpretation untouched.

Let us look in brief terms at the way meaning at the type level imposes constraints at the token level, remembering that in literature the token level *is* the poem, or the narrator or a character speaking inside a novel or a play. As it concerns analytic entailment, the process involves cases like those we have already discussed. *George had a nightmare* entails *George had a dream* as a matter of sense containment: *nightmare* literally "contains" *dream* as an element of its subordinate sense structure. By way of explaining a related feature of decompositional sense structure, I want to return to the problem that caused Wittgenstein to lose faith in the *Begriffsschrift* conception of language. Wittgenstein's dilemma, it will be recalled, is that the system developed in the *Tractatus* permitted no intelligible account of how "This object is blue," when asserted of an identical object at an identical time, contradicts "This object is red."

The basic problem is that denial or contradiction on the *Tractatus* system needs the negation sign, which is nowhere in sight in such examples. This limitation is what led to Wittgenstein's rather half-hearted speculations about "the logical structure of color," and ultimately to his turning his back on the *Tractatus* and picture theory in favor of the method used in *Philosophical Investigations*. For present purposes, the pertinent point is that in Katz's New Intensionalism, the problem of contradiction that so troubled Wittgenstein is very simply resolved through an account of superordination and then of antonymy relations among senses. The entire picture may be represented as follows (the diagram is mine, not Katz's):

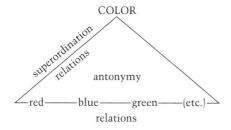

COLOR

superordination relations

antonymy

red———blue———green———(etc.)

relations

I shall explain antonymy relations below, but I want first to take a final look at superordination.

Superordination is at the heart of Katz's theory of decompositional sense structure. Its importance for literary theory is that it demonstrates in clear terms the intelligibility of a notion of literal meaning authorized, as Umberto Eco put it, "by the dullest and simplest of existing dictionaries." In Katz's terms, this is meaning at the type level, at which sense structure as a whole is controlled by superordination relations. So, for instance, when we think *furniture*, we really do think something like *physical object* at a superordinate level and things like *table* and *chair* and *couch* at a subordinate level of semantic entailment. (My use of "think" here implies a psychologism wholly foreign to Katz's theory. The reader will understand that I am using a shorthand.) This is Katz's whole point against Wittgenstein's claim that, since vagueness of meaning is very often the aim of an utterance—Wittgenstein's example is "The ground is quite covered with plants" (*PI* 70)—greater exactitude may be a mirage. For Katz, such "vagueness" simply equals respective levels of superordination. I may say "Pile some objects against the door," but I may *also* say "Pile some furniture against the door," "Pile some chairs against the door," "Pile some rocking chairs against the door," etc. (Katz's examples: *MM* 118).

The whole point of such examples is to show that *object* is "in" the sense structure of such terms or concepts as *furniture*, *chair*, and *rocking chair*, so that just as Wittgenstein, had he been moved to think from a decompositional standpoint, might have seen that *plant* may perfectly well entail—to go down the "tree" of permissible entailments—*bushes, rose bushes*, climbing tea-rose bushes, etc. To look at a syntactically simple expression like *chair* as it exists for the New Intensionalism will thus be, as in the semantic markers of chapter four, to see an "exploded" system of concepts and entailments, with superordination and antonymy relations sustaining the structure as a structure. The following is Katz's "standard" diagram of such relations. Assume that *chair* as the complex sense represented by c*:

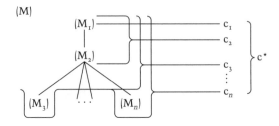

To see how Katz's diagram answers to our ordinary linguistic intuitions, it is only necessary to compare it with the ordinary dictionary definition of *chair*, which will normally consist of a serial list of descriptive and qualifying terms. In this case, Katz supplies a dictionary-like definition for purposes of his own: "a physical object which is a piece of furniture with a back and a seat, serving as a seat for one." The point of the diagram is then to permit the same definition to be seen in what might be called its three-dimensionality, with $c_1, c_2 \ldots c_n$ as the component concepts making up c*, c_1 representing the component sense "being an object," the branch connecting (M_1) to (M_2) representing the qualifying concept "being physical," and so on. Katz's point is that if such a formal representation is correct, the simple expression *chair* will be exactly synonymous with the cumbersome definition ("a physical object which is a piece of furniture," etc.) found in the dictionary.

For literary theory, especially at the level of primary or first-order meaning, the most important implication of Katz's intensional semantics is thus that we do not send our students to the OED to find definitions after all. For what was involved in discovering the meaning of *spheres* and *trepidation* and *moving of th'earth* in the handout in chapter one was really an exploration of underlying sense structure, entire systems and subsystems of concepts and entailments and superordination relations as they are at work beneath the surface of the words. This no doubt explains the otherwise uncanny sense, experienced sooner or later by every good close reader of literary texts, that one is at certain moments looking *into* the language rather than at it, that what can only be called a depth of semantic implication is somehow really there. On Katz's account of sense structure, it is there.

Katz's account of the type-token relation then permits an obvious explanation of the puzzle from which we began, which is why primary meaning operates as a trump in literary interpretation. For in literary theory there has always been a tendency to discuss literal meaning, in both ordinary discourse and literary works, as being something roughly equivalent to dictionary meaning. For Katz, on the other hand, dictionary meaning is not yet literal. It is simply a rough guide to sense structure as governed by syntactic and semantic rules at the type level. It is true that we could help a non-English-speaker to understand the meaning of "George is a fine friend" by pointing out the relevant sense of *friend* in a bilingual dictionary, but we could also illustrate *fine* by using it to refer to what we knew the non-English-speaker to recognize as exemplary instances of things: "Peter's Stradivarius is a fine violin," etc. For literal meaning in Katz's theory just is, as we have seen, what occurs when the senses of token and type coincide in the utterance context.

This rule of literal meaning might be called, with passing apologies to Tarski and Davidson, Katz's convention TT: "George is a fine friend" is literal iff the utterer means in the pragmatic context that George is a fine friend. (The expression "iff" here is logical shorthand for "if and only if.") The point for literary theory is that such a rule operates as a much tighter constraint in interpretation than in ordinary discourse. For in ordinary discourse, having heard that George burned down your house and ran off with your wife, I might well take "George is a fine friend" as non-literal, an ironic sentiment uttered in the bitterness of your heart. But should you then make clear that your house is still standing and your marriage blissful, and that the George you mean is someone who has just saved you from bankruptcy at great inconvenience to himself, I will see that I have gotten my stories mixed and that your meaning must be literal after all.

Katz leaves such possibilities as these open precisely because he wants to remain relatively uncommitted about pragmatic meaning—indeed, to deny in the name of a rigorous intensionalism that it is "meaning" at all. Yet in literary interpretation, where the pragmatic or extra-linguistic situation—the portrait in front of which the Duke and his listener are standing, the bronze sculpture of Neptune taming a seahorse, the party waiting downstairs for their conversation to conclude, etc.—is so to speak inside the language of the work, there is nothing that escapes the "top down" imposition of constraints as Katz describes it. The situation is thus one in which sense structure at the type level assumes an enormous power to determine meaning at all levels. This is what gives primary meaning its value as a trump.

Consider, one last time, Kerrigan's denial that Donne's *Elegy XIX* is a poem whose speaker, compelling a "submissive girl-victim" to do a strip tease act for him, mentions the massiveness of his own erection in the course of ordering her about. That is a description of an entire pragmatic or speech-act situation, but we are now in a position to understand why Kerrigan does not argue on the pragmatic level. His point against Carey's reading is, as we have seen, both simpler and more conclusive: (1) *massive* as Carey uses it has an obviously relevant sense at the type level, (2) there is nothing in the sense structure of any word or phrase in the poem corresponding to this sense, so that (3) it is impossible that Carey's reconstruction of the pragmatic situation—speaker/girl/strip tease—should then correspond *as a whole* to the dramatic situation actually portrayed in *Elegy XIX*. Thus an entire structure of second-order interpretation comes crashing down.

Yet Carey's fantasies about the massiveness of the speaker's erection are the sort of detail that, under different circumstances, a reading can get wrong and still survive. This is why the really conclusive part of Kerrigan's counterargument occurs when he directly confronts Carey on a point of textual implication: "Does one address a 'girl-victim' as 'Madame'?" This looks, if anything does, like an appeal to inference at the pragmatic level. One knows, when one hears "Madame," that one is hearing an address to a grown woman—for whom, in addition, the speaker presumably has a degree of respect—and one knows this in the same way that one makes certain similar inferences from hearing people addressed as, say, "your Majesty," "your honor," "sir," "mister," etc. An entire ratio between speaker and listener seems to be implied by such modes of address.

Yet Katz will insist that sense structure at the type level is involved even in such utterances as these—the argument is similar to the argument about naming given in chapter three—and that without an intensional theory there will be no way of accounting for pragmatic scatter as it occurs all the time in such cases. That is why we could imagine, for instance, a mother addressing a spoiled three-year-old as "your majesty" while picking up his toys yet again. To see this is to see that Kerrigan's argument from "Madame" is a great deal more complicated than it looks. It is, first of all, an argument about antonymy relations—as "blue" excludes "red" and "yellow," "Madame" here excludes such alternative forms as "Miss," "little girl," etc.—and then it is an argument that the pragmatic situation in *Elegy XIX* must be reconstructed around "Madame" taken in one way and not others.

In the case of *Elegy XIX*, this amounts to the claim that "Madame" as it establishes a ratio of speaker-listener address is to be taken as literal in precisely Katz's sense of type-token identity. For one can imagine all sorts of non-literal uses of "Madame" in roughly related contexts. If the speaker of Prior's wonderful little poem *To a Child of Quality Five Years Old* had addressed the fair Miss Mary this way, for instance, the implications would be altogether different. So Kerrigan's point, in terms of Katz's theory, is that any good reader can here see that in *this* instance of "Madame," type and token meaning coincide. Thus the simple use of "Madame" gives us a speaker celebrating the joys of sexual love with a woman to whom his relationship is at the same time intellectual, if only because he so obviously assumes her to be able to follow the complex play of his wit. Thus it is type meaning that has excluded what might be called the *Penthouse* reading here, even at what would ordinarily seem to be a purely pragmatic level of inference.

There is a further point. To see that sense structure at the type level sustains Kerrigan's reading and disallows that of Carey or Docherty— he, it will be recalled, of the girl-victim's "hymeneal boundary"—is to see that literal meaning on Katz's model imposes its constraints not only upon what we normally think of as the pragmatic situation, but then also upon what we might otherwise think of as matters of moral or normative judgment. For Kerrigan, in insisting that "Madame" establishes a certain pragmatic situation "inside" the poem, is also insisting on an entire set of values and attitudes implicit in that situation. So, for instance, "Madame" will *also* give us a listener who is there of her own free will, who shares the speaker's own sense of their love as a kind of private religion, and whose attitude towards sexual or physical love is, like his, free from the constraints of a more conventional morality. All these are values, and it is an implication of Katz's intensionalism that they, as much as the senses of individual words and sentences, are "in" the poem.

To have glimpsed this dimension of Kerrigan's argument is thus un-expectedly to see why such theorists of the New Criticism as Wimsatt and Beardsley and Brooks, usually thought of as apostles of close read-ing, always spoke of the theory of literary autonomy as essential to the New Criticism. At the time, this seemed puzzling. For literary au-tonomy, as was sometimes remarked, seemed a principle of rather higher generality than could be justified by a method that consisted, on the face of it, of little more than paying close attention to words and syntax. The connection was, I think, one that the New Critics them-selves grasped only intuitively, which is why there was a great deal of talk about Coleridgean organic unity, verbal icons and well-wrought urns, and very little directly relating close reading to the notion of poems like Donne's *Elegy XIX* or *Valediction: Forbidding Mourning* as worlds-in-themselves or separate spheres of reality.

Yet the simple case of Kerrigan's "Madame" permits one to see readily enough why this is a necessary connection. For if Kerrigan's way of taking "Madame" is right, we have not only the entire situation of utterance just described—the speaker and his love as souls who have freely and even joyously entered into the sexual relationship implied in the poem—but also the sense in which that situation exists as such by asserting its independence of a more conventional morality. In this sense, the meaning of the poem as a whole will be simply unavailable to a reader—even to a later John Donne, as it might be—who assumes that premarital or extramarital sex is at all times and under all circum-stances a sin against God and man and an invisible order of things. The celebratory sexuality of *Elegy XIX* is, in short, something like the prob-lem of the ghost in *Hamlet*. The literary work is its own world, and if as modern readers we allow our disbelief in ghosts to determine our view of reality at all times, we had better leave *Hamlet* on the shelf.

A traditional way of making this point was to say that, for the time one is reading *Hamlet*, the ghost upon the ramparts *is* real, an actual presence in a world where ghosts exist and operate to serious ends. In a work like Frye's *Anatomy of Criticism*, this was simply assumed to be a condition of literary comprehension. When one is reading the *Iliad* and the *Odyssey*, worlds where the Olympian gods and goddesses are as real as sun and rain, one has no right to object to Homer's poly-theism. One's own religious beliefs, or lack of them, are utterly irrele-vant. Nor does the polytheist or atheist or agnostic have the right to object to God and Satan and the angels when reading *Paradise Lost.* To Wimsatt—I am thinking now of his chapters of *Literary Criticism: A Short History*, written with Brooks—an intuition of literature as a separate reality was central to the entire tradition of western poetics from Aristotle through Sidney and Shelley to Wilde and T.S. Eliot.

At the time of *The Well Wrought Urn* or the *Anatomy of Criticism*, Kerrigan's insistence that "Madame" establishes *Elegy XIX* as one sort of pragmatic situation rather than another would simply have been taken as an insistence on its religion-as-love theme—on the poem's right to mean what it means, so to speak, against the strictures of any more conventional morality. Today, a similar insistence on primary meaning, in the rare instances when it is insisted on, will usually be an attempt to reclaim literary meaning from ideological or political interpretation. This is the sense in which Carey's notion that the poem is about a submissive girl-victim being made to perform a strip tease, or his related ruminations about males who inhabit a shadowland of pornographic fantasy—everything, in short, that Kerrigan's simple pointing to "Madame" brings crashing down—may be seen to draw its authority from a newer mode of ideological reading meant to demonstrate the complicity of literary works in one or another system of social domination.

In the current climate of Anglo-American literary studies, merely to mention this point is to raise various controversial issues. I have no desire to enter into them. My only point is that Kerrigan's particular mode of close reading must be counted in such a climate as resistance to the claims of political or ideological reading as such. The support such reading now unexpectedly gains from the New Intensionalism in semantic theory thus poses a new and significant obstacle to various contemporary modes of ideological interpretation. For the theory of literary autonomy associated by New Criticism with close reading and "the literary study of literature" was also the theory that literary works, as self-contained worlds embodying their own laws and their own logic, were subject to violence and distortion when made to answer to doctrines or epistemologies or ideologies external to themselves.

This is why Northrop Frye, for instance, whose *Anatomy of Criticism* was in many ways the summa of the formalist or New Critical program, was moved to argue in *The Educated Imagination* that the moral and intellectual value of literary studies lay in the way they demand tolerance as what might be called a methodological imperative. The Nazi or the Marxist or the Christian fundamentalist who permits him or herself wholly to enter and dwell in the world of the *Odyssey* or *The Divine Comedy* or *King Lear* must, Frye thought, come back to ordinary existence with at least some sense of their own deepest convictions as relative possibilities. It is not the least virtue of Katz's New Intensionalism, perhaps, that it allows one to see how writers like Frye could imagine themselves to be offering, in the place of the usual platitudes about great books and liberal education, a rigorous argument about the conditions of literary comprehension.

In recent years, as I shall briefly explain in the epilogue, Katz has come to see the greatest significance of his own semantic theory as lying in the way it points towards Platonism or linguistic realism at the ontological level. From this perspective, even readers unsympathetic to the claims of Katz's "metaphysics of meaning" will be interested in the way it provides new grounds of intelligibility for that deeper intuition of literary autonomy that Wimsatt saw as being central to western criticism from Aristotle to Wilde. For the notion that literature constitutes not only a separate but a timeless reality is something that one finds in literature itself almost from the beginning—Horace's *aere perennius*, Shakespeare's "Nor marble, nor gilded monuments"—and it is something that every serious student of literature understands, if only as a certain feeling or attitude, from personal experience. The sense that you and I and our physical surroundings will soon enough be dust, but that Hamlet will be there to greet other readers in another world two or three hundred years from now, can at times be very strong.

This notion of literature as a separate reality is what Aristotle had in mind, Frye thought, in saying that history only tells us what happened while poetry tells us what always happens. It is what Wimsatt took Sidney to have meant in saying that poetry gives us a golden world and nature only a brazen one, and Shelley to have in mind in calling poets the unacknowledged legislators of mankind. It is what Gilbert means, in Wilde's *The Critic as Artist*, in saying that Homer's is a world where Helen still comes every day out upon the battlements of Troy to gaze upon the fighting below, Achilles and Hector and Ajax and Paris as they issue forth to enter into mortal combat. "Phantoms, are they?" asks

Gilbert. "Heroes of mist and mountain? Shadows in a song? No: they are real. Action! What is action? It dies at the moment of its energy. . . . The world is made by the singer for the dreamer."

This is a vision, always before carrying mystical overtones despite its strange attractiveness—and despite the way it seems to answer to an intuition actually had by very many otherwise unmystical readers of Homer or Shakespeare or Dickens or Joyce—that becomes suddenly comprehensible in light of the ontological argument given by Katz in *The Metaphysics of Meaning*. What is timeless or real in the Platonic sense would on this argument not be the *Iliad* or the *Odyssey*, but Homeric Greek as a language that, though its last living speaker vanished from the earth some millennia ago, lives on today as a language for anyone who might want to learn it. For what one is learning when studying Homeric Greek would on Katz's account simply be to move in a world of timeless semantic possibility common to ourselves and the ancient Greeks and the speakers of languages yet to be born. It is of this world, and not our own, that the *Iliad* and *The Divine Comedy* and *King Lear* then live on as lasting monuments. In the epilogue, I shall say a word about why Katz sees this ontology of language to be the most important implication of his New Intensionalism.

Epilogue : The Metaphysics of Meaning

The most controversial aspect of Katz's New Intensionalism is his linguistic realism, or, to use a term he no longer fully accepts, his Platonism. This is the position that grammar and meaning in such natural languages as French and German and Sanskrit draw continuously on a realm of pure semantic possibility existing outside space and time, in much the way numbers and geometric figures are thought to exist by mathematical realists. This realm is the domain of Katz's *senses*, which are not only mind-independent but language-independent entities. One readily enough sees why the position is controversial. I may, with a bit of effort, think of what I mean by this sentence as having an existence apart from my mind. To think of that meaning as existing apart from the *language* I am using, however, puts a greater strain on ordinary intuition.

To see why Katz moved toward a realist position in semantic theory, to the point where realist epistemology now counts as his main philosophical interest, it is useful to trace the path he has taken since his early days as a Chomskyan generative grammarian. For Katz did not start out as a linguistic realist. To the contrary, his early paper "Mentalism in Linguistics," defending the view that linguistics is the study of the psychological structure of human language learners, is still quoted as a classic of the opposing position. The notion of linguistics as a psychological study is one to which Chomsky himself has adhered throughout his career. I shall explain in a moment why Chomsky's notion of linguistic competence raises problems that Katz began to see as irresolvable, thus moving him in a realist direction, but it will be well to begin with the way Chomsky himself viewed the issue at the time he wrote *Aspects of the Theory of Syntax*:

> Linguistic theory is concerned primarily with an ideal speaker-listener, in a completely homogeneous speech-community, who

knows its language perfectly, and is unaffected by such grammatically irrelevant conditions as memory limitations, distractions, shifts of attention and interest, and errors (random or characteristic) in applying his knowledge of the language in actual performance. . . . We thus make a fundamental distinction between *competence* (the speaker-hearer's knowledge of his language) and *performance* (the actual use of language in concrete situations). (3–4)

The dominant model at the moment Chomsky grasped the possibility of generative grammar, it will be remembered, was Bloomfieldian structuralism. Bloomfield himself, together with such influential linguists as Chomsky's own teacher Zelig Harris, had imposed on the study of language a set of severely nominalistic constraints. The linguist was to forswear any loose metaphysical notions of "meanings" or "ideas" and study samples of language as acoustical patterns or ink or pencil marks, cataloguing the distributional regularities as one encountered them. (They really meant this: such was the price of being "properly scientific" in the days of the verification principle.) Language, we have heard Bloomfield say, is the study of a certain kind of noise.

It is important to see what the *idea* of language study dictated by this conception looks like. Imagine that you are an anthropologist from a culture in which chess is wholly unknown. You have been given the task of figuring out what it is that people in chess-playing cultures do when they play. Your procedure is simple: you go to chess tournaments and, with a notebook in your hand, you observe the activities being carried out with the physical objects used by the participants. There always seem to be eight of the smallest objects used by each participant, for instance, and two each of some of the others, and one each of still others. The activity is carried out on a flat surface divided into rectangles. By tabulating the rectangles and indexing each of the objects, you begin to develop a distributional account of the way the position of the objects is altered in the activity.

Now it is appealing in this situation to think that, once you had catalogued enough regularities, you would somehow "arrive inductively" at the rules of chess. But this is not the case. The idea is attractive precisely because, reading this now, you *know* the rules of chess—or, if you do not, you know that there are such rules—and imagine that they are so to speak there waiting to be discovered on a purely statistical account of regularities. Try, though, to imagine the scene as it really would look to you as an anthropologist who does not even know that "rules" are involved. The point is that a distributional regularity is not a rule. The baseball player who *invariably* taps the dirt off his spikes before stepping into the batter's box is not obeying a rule, but no purely distributional account of his activity will reveal the difference between the non-rule-governed activity (dirt tapping) and the rule-governed activity (stepping into the batter's box).

To even try to imagine this sort of situation is to see why Chomsky's notion of generative grammar seemed so liberating. For what corresponds to the knights and bishops of the chess example are the verbs and nouns and grammatical rules of ordinary speech: a finite system of elements able to generate a virtual infinity of games or, in the case of language, meaningful utterances. Furthermore, Chomsky insisted that a strong linguistic theory would account for these as operating in a "top down" way. Where the taxonomic grammar of Bloomfield committed linguists to a "bottom up" approach—exactly like the anthropologist who walks into a chess tournament with nothing but a notebook and the bare idea of statistical distribution—Chomsky's theory put the linguist in the position of an anthropologist who, so to speak, walks into the tournament knowing in advance that there are rules of chess.

The revolution began with Chomsky's notion of a system of grammatical rules that would generate all and only the grammatical sentences in a language. The question was: what interpretation was one to give the theory now that one had it? One was no longer studying language as noise, but what, exactly, *was* one studying? Chomsky's answer, as we have heard, is that the linguist studies language competence—a capacity to learn language that is somehow built into the neurons and synapses of the human brain. To go back to Chomsky's early writings on language acquisition is immediately to see why this idea is attractive. For human children do, obviously, come equipped with some system that permits them to internalize the rules governing utterance and comprehension. Just as obviously, there is something universal about this capacity. A two-year-old raised in France will learn French, but the same two-year-old transported to China will just as readily learn Chinese.

Why, then, not simply say that linguistics is a study of linguistic competence? The problem begins with the notion of idealization. For a system of generative grammar will be no good, every Chomskyan agreed, if it generates ungrammatical as well as grammatical sentences. On the other hand, the idea of grammaticality then seems to presuppose a notion of competence: sentences do not come prelabeled grammatical or ungrammatical, and the linguist needs some means of distinguishing between *Very the hot side, rain tantrum zoo* and *I'm going to the store later if it doesn't rain.* The obvious thing to do in this situation, Chomskyan linguists saw readily enough, is to check sentences generated by the grammar against the intuitions of competent native speakers.

Now, however, a circularity enters. Since we don't want *ungrammatical* speakers as umpires—someone who has grown up in another linguistic culture and speaks our language imperfectly, say, or someone who has suffered neurological damage in an automobile accident—we have to have some standard for deciding their competence in advance. And the standard we want is whether they speak grammatically or not. The same thing holds for the data studied by the linguist: in collecting sentences for which we attempt to construct rules, we don't want sentences uttered by people who are drunk, or who have just taken LSD, or who are unable to speak intelligibly because they recently had a stroke. All this is part of what Chomsky means in speaking of "an ideal speaker-listener, in a completely homogeneous speech-community, who knows its language perfectly."

The reason that Chomsky himself has never seen a problem of circularity here is that he has always thought of the idealization as being a version of idealization in the physical sciences. That is, just as the physicist who wants to account for the laws governing the movement of objects posits a ball moving across a frictionless plane, the linguist posits something like Chomsky's ideal speaker-listener in accounting for the underlying rules of grammar that govern human utterance. So the object of study in linguistics really is something like the LAD or Language Acquisition Device posited in Chomsky's early speculations about linguistic competence, except that it is this device under a suitably idealized description.

The problem here is, as Katz saw, that no idealization of a *mechanism* for learning language can account for such properties as grammaticality, meaningfulness, and numerous others to which the Chomskyan linguist is committed by the very notion of a formal representation of grammatical rules. An essential insight here comes from the study of logic, where the same issue has been debated over a longer period of time. For everyone agrees that logic in some sense concerns "laws of thought": it is the way one *must* reason if one wishes to reason validly. The question is: how is one to conceive of "laws"? If we imagine logical truth as belonging to some timeless realm of *a priori* truth there are some philosophical problems, but none about what we mean by "law." For on this interpretation valid reason simply becomes agreement with certain mind-independent principles of implication and entailment.

Yet the notion of a timeless realm of logical truth has seemed insupportably metaphysical to some philosophers. Human beings are spatio-temporal creatures, and their knowledge comes by direct acquaintance with spatio-temporal objects. It is not clear how it could be meaningful even to say that one had contact with a realm outside space and time—in logic, in mathematics, or in language—let alone how one could say that part of one's knowledge came from such contact. There have been various attempts to construct alternative accounts, but the one relevant here is the notion that logical truth is "true" in a purely psychological sense. That is, the brain is so constructed that when one has an *a*-type thought ("All men are mortal") in conjunction with a *b*-type thought ("Socrates is a man"), there is then a neural connection that automatically generates a *c*-type thought ("Socrates is mortal").

For Katz, the conclusive response to this sort of speculation was Frege's. For as Frege saw, any attempt to account for logical validity in terms of a "logic organ" built into the human brain would then have to be ready for the discovery that some people's organs generated different sorts of connections than others. What would one do, in short, if one were discover an island whose inhabitants reasoned as follows: *All horses have four legs; The animal on which I am riding is a horse; Therefore, the animal on which I am riding has three legs?* Here is Frege:

> . . . what if beings were ever found whose laws of thought flatly contradicted ours and therefore led to contrary results even in practice? The psychological logician could only acknowledge the fact and say simply: those laws hold for them, these laws hold for us. I should say: we have here a hitherto unknown type of mad-

ness. Anyone who understands laws of logic to be laws that prescribe the way in which one ought to think— . . . and not natural laws of human beings taking a thing to be true—will ask, who is right? . . . The psychological logician cannot ask this question: if he did he would be recognizing laws of truth that were not laws of psychology. (qtd. in *LOAO* 171)

Husserl had a similar argument about trying to imagine logical truth as a product of psychological laws. One of his points bears directly on Chomsky's competencism in linguistics. It is—to use a terminology not available to Husserl—that even a brain constructed to give nothing but logically valid results would not show that logical truth was identical to neural connections. "Let us imagine an ideal person," said Husserl, "in whom *all* thinking proceeds as logical laws require. Naturally the fact that this occurs must have its explanatory ground in certain psychological laws, which govern the course of the mental experiences of this being. . . . I now ask: Would the natural laws and the logical laws in this assumed situation be one and the same? Obviously the answer is 'No'" (qtd. in *LOAO* 174).

In an age of hand calculators and computers, it is easy enough to see the point Husserl is making here. First, if we see that *this* brain is invariably coming to logically valid conclusions, just as we might see that *this* calculator always gives correct results to multiplication problems, it must be because we have an independent notion of logical validity—or multiplication rules—by which to judge the results. Nor will it do, in the manner of Chomskyan idealization, to say that we obtained our standard by idealizing away from the imperfections of actual reasoners or actual hand calculators, for then there will arise the question of how we knew what constituted an "imperfection" in any earlier case. The second point is that, even when calculators do invariably give correct results, we are not disposed to say that the laws of arithmetic are identical with the operations of the device. What we are disposed to say is that engineers have found a way to instantiate the rules of arithmetic in a system of wires and microchips. This does not make the study of arithmetic a study of microchip circuitry.

Katz does not want to deny that brains really have been set up to handle both logic and language, or that there are mental processes involved in their doing so, or anything else that is obviously true about the way I use the laws of logic to reason or the rules of grammar to speak. His point is simply that the laws of logic and the rules of grammar are *what* I use in such cases, and always have an existence separate from the various faculties and mental processes that might come into play when I do make use of them. To see linguistics as the study of a Language Acquisition Device, or a "language organ," or a "psycho-grammar," is on Katz's view simply to miss the essential distinction between my knowing something—a language, the rules of a game, the code of dress for formal occasions—and the something it is knowledge of.

Katz's linguistic realism begins here. To see "language" as the object of study in linguistics, as commonsensical as that no doubt sounds, is to begin to conceive of it as a purely abstract system of rules and meanings. This is what happened to Katz as a result of his early criticisms of Chomsky's competencism. He saw very clearly that for the reasons just given linguistics could *not* be the study of human neurobiology, or LADS or psychogrammars, but it has taken him twenty years of systematic work in semantic theory to work through the implications of seeing Language—I now use the capital L to refer specifically to Katz's realist conception of language—as the true object of study in linguistics.

To try to think in any immediate terms about Language as existing in a timeless realm apart from ordinary existence is to raise the philosophical problem mentioned earlier: if grammatical rules and linguistic meanings exist outside space and time, how is it possible for spatio-temporal creatures like ourselves to have any contact with them, let alone to use them to communicate with each other? (As we shall shortly see, this is just the problem that confronts the mathematical realist: it may very well be that numbers are abstract objects existing outside space and time, but then how do we use them to count apples and measure patios for bricklaying jobs?) In recent years, Katz has been concentrating more and more on trying to solve this problem on a purely epistemological level. I shall summarize his conclusions below, but I want first to spend a moment on Katz's earlier approach to solving the problem *within* semantic theory.

We have discussed Katz's interpretation of the type-token relation primarily as it involves the concept of pragmatic scatter. At this practical level, what is noteworthy about the type-token relation is that it seems straightforwardly and uncontroversially methodological. It is hard to imagine an account of meaning that would not, if only as a working distinction, somehow take note of the fact that my utterance of the word *blue* or *barn* or *the* cannot be identical with those words as they exist in English as a linguistic system apart from my utterance. Here, once again, is C. S. Peirce: "There will ordinarily be about twenty 'the's on a page, and of course they count as twenty words. In another sense of the word 'word,' however, there is but one 'the' in English language; . . . it is impossible that this word should lie visibly on a page or be heard in any voice" (qtd. in *MM* 39).

There is in this clearly a tendency towards Language in Katz's realist sense. A "word" that cannot appear on any page or be heard in any voice must in some sense exist in a Platonic realm apart from real speakers and actual conversations. But it is important to see, at the same time, how purely commonsensical a matter this is. For we are only dealing here with something like Saussure's distinction between *langue* and *parole*. I am aware, if I think about it, that English existed as a language before I was born, and that it will continue to exist when I am dead. It would have existed had I never been born. So language must, to at least that extent, have an existence apart from me as a speaker. But then this will be true of any conversation I have with you: it might never have taken place, just as you or I might never have existed, but the language that made our utterance possible would have existed.

The distinction, in short, is between a world of pure contingency—the world into which I might or might not have been born, the world in which this or that conversation might or might not have taken place—and a realm about which, so far, all one need say is that it is not identical with that contingent world. In linguistic terms, a great deal hangs on the distinction. To say that "It's raining outside" is a meaningful utterance is precisely to say that each of the words inside the quotes is a token in Peirce's sense, bearing an essential relation to other words—in Katz's theory, to an entire system of grammatical rules and abstract senses at the type level—that do not appear on the page, or any page. To say otherwise, and mean it, is quite literally to reduce the ink marks inside the quotes to nothing *but* ink marks: "@#." (This I take to be the point of Wittgenstein's "*Say* xyz and *mean* 'The weather is going to be fine.'")

On my own view, as I remarked in the preface, the notion of type meaning as simply existing "elsewhere" than token meaning, even if this were taken as a methodological fiction, would give Katz's interpretation of the type-token relation momentous implications for literary theory. For that interpretation, as I have tried to show, permits a full account of determinate meaning within the literary work considered as a type of complex speech act. But it is also easy enough to see why Katz, having arrived at such an interpretation in support of his own realist intuitions in semantic theory, should then have been led by the notion of type meaning in the direction of an even more radical linguistic realism. For consider how willing even Quine, who was Katz's great opponent in the early debates over analyticity and synonymy, has been to acknowledge the distinction between type and token:

> ER IST DER GEIST DER SICH DEN KORPER BAUT: such is the nine-word inscription on a Harvard museum. The count is nine because we count *der* both times; we are counting concrete physical objects, nine in a row. When on the other hand statistics are compiled regarding students' vocabularies, a firm line is drawn at repetitions: no cheating. Such are two contrasting senses in which we use the word *word*. A word in the second sense is not a physical object, not a dribble of ink or an incision in granite, but an abstract object. In the second sense of the word *word* it is not two words *der* that turn up in the inscription, but one word *der* that gets inscribed twice. Words in the first sense have come to be called *tokens*; words in the second sense are called *types*. (*Quiddities*, 216–17)

With Quine's notion of words as abstract objects, we find ourselves suddenly in the timeless world of linguistic meaning that Katz has been mapping with ever greater exactitude since he published *Language and Other Abstract Objects* in 1981. As we have seen, it is a world that, by the time we get to *The Metaphysics of Meaning*, includes *senses* that must be understood as existing prior to and independent of the words of any actual language. On a first approximation, these are what we have in mind when we say that *Es regnet* and *Il pleut* and *It's raining* all mean "the same thing." In Katz's later semantic theory they are what comes to mind when we realize not only that natural languages come and go in human history, but that anything we should want to call a natural language, though it might well not express the same senses as our own, would necessarily take the same means of expressing them.

The major intuition of Katz's New Intensionalism at this level is very close to that sustaining mathematical realism. Katz in recent years has moved more and more into philosophy of mathematics to demonstrate that his own realism is simply a variant of the Platonism of such mathematicians as G. H. Hardy and Kurt Gödel. The great parable of such mathematical Platonism is the twice-told tale of Hardy's bedside conversation with Ramanujan. Srinvasa Ramanujan, as most readers will be aware, was the Indian genius who, living in a poor district of Madras, "invented" a great deal of higher mathematics by himself after reading a single textbook. The letter he sent introducing himself to Hardy, page after scrawled page of strange and brilliant mathematical discoveries, has itself become a legend. The taxi-cab story is from the period after Ramanujan, with Hardy's support, had made his way to England. It is here retold by C. P. Snow in his foreword to a standard edition of Hardy's *Apology*:

> Hardy used to visit him, as he lay dying in hospital at Putney. It was on one of those visits that there happened the incident of the taxi-cab number. Hardy had gone out to Putney by taxi, as usual his chosen method of conveyance. He went into the room where Ramanujan was lying. Hardy, always inept about introducing a conversation, said, probably without a greeting, and certainly as his first remark: "I thought the number of my taxi-cab was 1729. It seemed to me rather a dull number." To which Ramanujan replied: "No, Hardy! It is a very interesting number. It is the smallest number expressible as the sum of two cubes in two different ways." (37)

The point of the story, for the mathematical Platonist, is that the number 1729, as well as the set of mathematical properties and relations instantly adduced by Ramanujan, are so obviously real to both parties to the conversation—as real, one wants to say, as the taxi-cab in which Hardy was carried to the hospital. This is a note that enters again and again when working mathematicians are talking among themselves, and mathematical realism might be described as simply an attempt to state as an ontological position what seems to them intuitively self-evident. The same point is often made by pointing to simultaneous discoveries of mathematical truth, as with Leibnitz and Newton's independent discovery of the differential calculus, or, indeed, Ramanujan's own discovery, working in solitude in poverty-stricken surroundings in Madras, of solutions to various problems on which Hardy was at work in England. This is what Hardy is trying to get across in saying, as we have heard, that he believes that "mathematical reality lies outside us, that our function is to discover or *observe* it, and that the theorems which we prove . . . are simply our notes of our observations" (qtd. In *LOAO* 22–23).

To grant Katz the same sort of point about linguistic reality would therefore be simply to extend to language an epistemological realism already common enough, if not universally accepted, in logic and mathematics. And, indeed, Katz's ultimate point will be that these all belong to the same domain. This can be taken to explain, for instance, why Russell and Whitehead were able to think of arithmetic as being a special application of the laws of logic, or why logical entailments of the *George had a nightmare* ——→ *George had a dream* sort, which we have seen to play a major role in Katz's New Intensionalism, are so obviously at work in language. Herein lies, so to speak, the good news for Katz's linguistic realism. The bad news is that it is then open to the same objections as mathematical and logical realism.

The classic summary of these objections is Paul Benacerraf's paper "Mathematical Truth," which concludes that, taken together, existing accounts of mathematical truth and mathematical knowledge seem to exclude any possibility of realist epistemology. The paper covers a great deal of technical ground that cannot be summarized here, but the point that comes to bear most directly on Katz's realism, one I have already mentioned, is not technical. It is that we are spatio-temporal creatures, physical bodies living among physical objects, and that knowledge comes to us through our senses. It is coherent to say that I have knowledge of the tables and chairs in my surroundings because I keep bumping into them. ("Bumping" may here be taken as a shorthand for what philosophers call the causal theory of knowledge.) But how can we, existing *inside* space and time, have any contact with objects like prime numbers or Katz's linguistic senses, which a realist like Katz himself describes as existing *outside* space and time?

It is important to see that the puzzle here is not just one about ontology—that is, about whether that "mathematical reality" we have heard Hardy describe really exists in some realm outside space and time. It is that *even if it did exist*, we could not on a causal account of knowledge know how things stood there. For such abstract objects as prime numbers and Katz's senses have the property, *even on the description of such realists as Hardy and Katz,* of being what epistemologists call causally inert. Benacerraf's way of putting this is to say that "the connection between the truth conditions for the statements of number theory and any relevant events connected with people who are supposed to have mathematical knowledge cannot be made out," because, as he arrestingly says, our "four dimensional space-time worm does not make the necessary contact" with mathematical reality (qtd. in *RR* 27).

The same notion lies behind most attempts to come up with non-realist accounts of mathematical knowledge. If it is impossible that we should have any sort of natural acquaintance with mathematical objects, then any knowledge we might claim to have of them would have to come from some mystical or supernatural contact. Realists like Hardy and Gödel and Katz, says Hartry Field, are "going to have to postulate some *aphysical connection,* some *mysterious grasping.*" The appeal of mathematicians like Gödel to knowledge through intuition, says Charles Chihara, "is like appealing to experiences vaguely described as 'mystical experiences' to justify belief in the existence of God" (qtd. in *RR* 32). To posit prime numbers or linguistic senses as having a real existence outside space and time is, in short, not simply to talk nonsense but to indulge in superstition and mysticism.

Against this line of reasoning Katz makes a highly original move, so much so that one cannot yet tell what the effect on standard epistemological arguments is going to be. For Katz's point is that every influential posing of the "problem of mathematical knowledge" to date has assumed empiricism and the causal theory of knowledge as the standard of *all* meaningful knowledge, and that nothing *in* the empiricist arguments justify doing so. To put the matter in oversimplified terms: we grow up in a world where our earliest sense of external reality comes from bumping into tables and chairs. Then, this notion having established itself as a standard, we extrapolate it to other kinds of knowledge—e.g., cloud chambers in physics or electron microscopes in chemistry—that can be construed in similar terms. Then, having stretched the notion of causal contact as far as it will seemingly go, we draw an invisible circumference around the farthest limit and declare that nothing exists outside that circumference, or that if it did, we should have no means of knowing it was there.

The point, of course, is that there is a deep incoherence written into this situation at the outset. Nobody doubts that, in a world of tables and chairs, a certain kind of reliable knowledge may come from bumping into them, but it is not then clear why this knowledge should be made the standard of *all* knowledge, and least of all that which involves objects—prime numbers, equilateral triangles, linguistic senses on Katz's account—that one cannot bump into. This is not, on Katz's part, some sort of generalized philosophical scepticism of the Cartesian or "how do I know that anything at all exists?" variety. His point is simply that anyone who wanted to establish the causal theory of knowledge as a standard for all meaningful knowledge needs to tell us *why* it should have this privileged status, and moreover to do so in a way that does not simply assume the validity of the causal theory, which would make argument circular. And this, as Katz points out, nobody has done.

The effect of Katz's latest work on mathematical realism is a kind of grand sweeping of the board, something like the analogy Wittgenstein once drew between philosophical puzzlement and being shut in a room: one tries the window and it is locked; one looks up the chimney and it is too narrow to climb; one tries to pry up a floorboard and it is too firmly fastened. The one thing one doesn't do is turn around and look at the door, which has been open all the time. For to review the existing philosophical literature on "the problem of mathematical knowledge" is to see that every important anti-realist argument to date really has, in one way or another, silently assumed the validity of the causal theory: we are spatio-temporal creatures, and *therefore we can only know objects through causal connection*, and numbers are on a realist account causally inert, so how could there be any contact between us and them?

There is a further point. The notion that real knowledge must consist in some sort of direct perception is so powerful that it has influenced realists as much as anti-realists, leading to serious claims that numbers and other abstract entities may be the objects of a certain kind of perception. When an anti-realist like Field talks impatiently about the way in which a realist account of mathematics seems to involve some sort of *"aphysical connection,* some *mysterious grasping,"* for instance, what clearly offends him is the incoherence of the claim that objects that cannot be perceived—i.e., seen, heard, touched—are nonetheless somehow being perceived. But make this same sort of mysterious grasping or aphysical connection into a positive philosophical doctrine and suddenly you are dealing not with an anti-realist but with Plato, the most famous realist in the history of philosophy, and the idea that there is a timeless world of archetypes or ideal forms that may, nonetheless, somehow be perceived by human beings.

Katz's recent work in epistemology and the philosophy of mathematics is complex and suggestive, an entire subject unto itself, and I shall not attempt to summarize it here. I shall simply end by saying that Katz now thinks that abstract objects like numbers and linguistic senses belong, as much as tables and chairs and trees and mountains, to what might be called the furniture of the ordinary world, and that the key to realist epistemology lies in seeing that our way of coming to know them bears *no* relation to the way we perceive or make inferences about physical objects. Yet so powerful is the empiricist model that we have, as yet, no vocabulary for knowledge that does not involve perception, unless it were some vocabulary of mystical or "mysterious grasping," which Katz rejects in terms as peremptory as an anti-realist like Field.

Developing a vocabulary that will permit him to express the central insights of his newest epistemological realism will be, one suspects, Katz's primary task in the immediate future. For those who have followed his thinking over the last ten or fifteen years, the rewards of seeing where his project will take him next will be very great. For those whose main interest is in literary studies, however, and in literature itself as an order of meaning as worthy of serious study as galaxies or subatomic particles or the structure of DNA, it is the work completed by Katz between *Language and Other Abstract Objects* and *The Metaphysics of Meaning* that will most clearly be seen to suggest a new and productive direction for literary theory. I've tried in the previous pages to give some sense of what that work looks like in its main outlines. My hope is that some readers, at least, will see in it, as do I, the promise of restoring literary studies to the status of a genuine discipline.

Works Cited

Note: quotations in the text from Wittgenstein's *Tractatus* are by proposition number, quotations from the *Philosophical Investigations* by section number. My parenthetical references to certain works are given in shorthand form. In these cases, the brackets following the items below are guides to the references. Items included in the bibliography but not cited in the text are assumed by my discussion at one or another point.

Armstrong, D. *The Nature of Mind.* Ithaca NY: Cornell University Press, 1981.

Austin, J. L. *How to Do Things with Words.* Cambridge: Harvard University Press, 1962.

Beardsley, M. C. *The Possibility of Criticism.* Detroit: Wayne State University Press, 1967.

Bloomfield, L. *Language.* New York: Henry Holt, 1933.

———. "Language or Ideas?" *Language* 12 (1936): 89–95.

Brooks, C. *The Well Wrought Urn.* New York: Harcourt, Brace, 1947.

Brooks, C., and R. P. Warren. *Understanding Poetry.* New York: Henry Holt, 1938.

Brower, R. A. *The Fields of Light.* New York: Oxford University Press, 1951.

Brower, R. A., and R. Poirier. *In Defense of Reading.* New York: E. P. Dutton, 1962.

Carroll, L. *Alice in Wonderland.* 2nd ed. Ed. Donald J. Gray. New York: W. W. Norton, 1992.

Carnap, R. *Meaning and Necessity.* Chicago: University of Chicago Press, 1956.

———. *The Logical Syntax of Language.* London: Routledge & Kegan Paul, 1937.

Chomsky, N. *Aspects of the Theory of Syntax.* Cambridge: MIT Press, 1966.

———. "The Current Scene in Linguistics." In *Topics in the Theory of Generative Grammar.* The Hague: Mouton, 1966.

———. *Knowledge of Language: Its Nature, Origin, and Use.* New York: Praeger, 1985.

Church, A. "Intensional Isomorphism and Identity of Belief." *Philosophical Studies* 5 (1954): 65–73.

Davidson, D. *Inquiries into Truth and Interpretation.* Oxford: Clarendon Press, 1985.

Donnellan, K. "Reference and Definite Descriptions." *Philosophical Review* 75 (1966): 261–304.

Dowling, W. C. *The Critic's Hornbook: Reading for Interpretation*. New York: Thomas Y. Crowell, 1977.

———. "Intentionless Meaning." In *Against Theory*, ed. W. J. T. Mitchell. Chicago: University of Chicago Press, 1985.

Eco, U. *The Limits of Interpretation*. Bloomington: Indiana University Press, 1994.

Fish, S. *Is There a Text in this Class?* Cambridge: Harvard University Press, 1980. [*TITC*]

Fodor, J. A. *The Language of Thought*. New York: Thomas Y. Crowell, 1975.

———. *Psychosemantics*. Cambridge: MIT Press, 1987.

Fodor, J. D. *Semantics: Theories of Meaning in Generative Grammar*. New York: Harper and Row, 1977.

Frege, G. *Conceptual Notation and Related Articles*. Oxford: Oxford University Press, 1972.

Frye, N. *The Anatomy of Criticism*. Princeton NJ: Princeton University Press, 1957.

———. *The Educated Imagination*. Bloomington: Indiana University Press, 1964.

Grice, H. P. *Studies in the Way of Words*. Cambridge: Harvard University Press, 1989.

Hardy, G. H. *A Mathematician's Apology*. With a foreword by C. P. Snow. Cambridge, England: Cambridge University Press, 1994.

Harris, Z. *Methods of Structural Linguistics*. Chicago: University of Chicago Press, 1951.

Kant, Immanuel. *Critique of Pure Reason*. Trans. N. K. Smith. New York: Humanities Press, 1929.

Katz, J. J. *Cogitations*. Oxford: Oxford University Press, 1986.

———. "Common Sense in Semantics." In *New Directions in Semantics*, ed. E. LePore. London: Academic Press, 1987.

———. "Has the Description Theory of Names Been Refuted?" In *Meaning and Method*, ed. G. Boolos. Cambridge, England: Cambridge University Press, 1990.

———. *Language and Other Abstract Objects*. Totowa NJ: Rowman and Littlefield, 1981. [*LOAO*]

———. *The Metaphysics of Meaning*. Cambridge: MIT Press, 1990. [*MM*]

———. "Names Without Bearers." *The Philosophical Review* 103 (1994): 1–39.

———. *Propositional Structure and Illocutionary Force*. Cambridge: Harvard University Press, 1980.

———. *Realistic Rationalism*. Cambridge: MIT Press, 1998. [*RR*]

———. *Semantic Theory*. New York: Harper and Row, 1972.

Katz, J. J., C. Leacock, and Y. Ravin. "A Decompositional Theory of Modification." In *Actions and Events*, ed. E. LePore and B. McLaughlin. Oxford: Basil Blackwell, 1986.

Kerrigan, W. "Seventeenth-Century Studies." In *Redrawing the Boundaries: The Transformation of English and American Literary Studies*. Ed. S. Greenblatt and G. Gunn. New York: Modern Language Association, 1992.

Kripke, S. *Naming and Necessity.* Cambridge: Harvard University Press, 1980.

Langendoen, D. T. and P. Postal. *The Vastness of Natural Languages.* Oxford: Oxford University Press, 1984.

Levvis, G. W. "Wittgenstein's Grammatical Propositions as Linguistic Exemplars: A Refutation of Katz's Semantic Platonism," *Philosophical Investigations* 19 (1996).

Lewis, D. *Convention.* Cambridge: Harvard University Press, 1969.

———. *Counterfactuals.* Oxford: Basil Blackwell, 1973

———. *On the Plurality of Worlds.* Oxford: Basil Blackwell, 1986.

Maddy, P. *Realism in Mathematics.* Oxford: Clarendon Press, 1990.

McGinn, C. *Wittgenstein on Meaning.* Oxford: Basil Blackwell, 1984.

Marcus, R. B. *Modalities: Philosophical Essays.* New York: Oxford University Press, 1993.

Matthews, R. "Troubles with Representationalism." *Social Research* 51 (1984).

Pavel, T. *Fictional Worlds.* Cambridge: Harvard University Press, 1986.

Polanyi, M. *Personal Knowledge: Towards a Post-Critical Philosophy.* Chicago: University of Chicago Press, 1974.

Popper, K. R. *Objective Knowledge.* London: Oxford University Press, 1972.

Putnam, H. "The Meaning of 'Meaning.'" *Language, Mind, and Knowledge: Minnesota Studies in the Philosophy of Science.* Vol. 7. Ed. K. Gunderson. Minneapolis: University of Minnesota Press, 1979.

———. "It Ain't Necessarily So." *Journal of Philosophy* 59 (1962): 658–671.

———. "Is Semantics Possible?" *Metaphilosophy* 1 (1970): 187–201.

Quine, W. V. O. *From a Logical Point of View.* Cambridge: Harvard University Press, 1961. [*LPV*]

———. *Ontological Relativity and Other Essays.* New York: Columbia University Press, 1969.

———. *The Ways of Paradox.* New York: Random House, 1966.

———. *Word and Object.* Cambridge: MIT Press, 1960.

———. *Quiddities.* Cambridge: Harvard University Press, 1987.

Radford, A. *Transformational Grammar.* Cambridge, England: Cambridge University Press, 1988.

Searle, J. R. *Speech Acts.* Cambridge, England: Cambridge University Press, 1969.

Van Ghent, Dorothy. *The English Novel.* New York: Holt, Rinehart, and Winston, 1953.

Wimsatt, W. K., and M. C. Beardsley. *The Verbal Icon.* Lexington: University of Kentucky Press, 1954.

Wittgenstein, L. *Philosophical Investigations.* Oxford: Basil Blackwell, 1953.

———. *Tractatus Logico-Philosophicus.* Trans. D. F. Pears and B. F. McGuiness. London: Routledge & Kegan Paul, 1961.

Index

second-order interpretation, xiv, 3; as derived from primary meaning, xii, 91; as unmoored from primary meaning in contemporary criticism, 14

sense: as determining reference, 22, 48–49

senses: as abstract entities, 2, 16–17, 71, 107; as language-independent entities, 99

Shakespeare, William, xi, 96–97

Shelley, Percy Bysshe, 95–96

Sidney, Sir Philip, 95–96

Sinn and *Bedeutung*, 44, 46–48, 53

Snow, C. P., 108

Sophocles, xi

speech acts, 15, 78, 93; poem as, 83, 88; literary work as, 88

substitution procedure, 63; illustrated, 62

Superman, 45

superordination, 33–34, 72, 75–76, 89–90

synonymy, 36, 41, 43

tacit dimension (Polanyi), x

Tarski, Alfred, 91

taxonomic grammar, 38, 61–62, 101

theoretical entities in language, 32

theory: English departments' conception of, 79

top-down model of grammar and meaning, 19, 21, 67, 83, 92, 101

tragedy, xi

trifling propositions, 35

type-token relation, 17, 21–22, 27, 44, 52, 82–85, 87–88, 91, 105, 107; defined, 20

universal grammar, 67–68, 70

use-mention distinction, 52

Van Ghent, Dorothy, 87

Venus: as Morning Star and Evening Star, 45–48

Warren, Austin, 3

Whitehead, Alfred North, 109

Wilde, Oscar, 95–96

Wimsatt, W. K., xi, 3, 94–96

Wittgenstein, Ludwig, 15, 18, 20–26, 27–30, 32–33, 35–36, 40, 42–43, 53, 55–60, 65, 71, 80–89, 106

Wordsworth, William, xi

Wug, 62–63